Wisdom and Age

John-Raphael Staude

Editor

Ross Books
P.O.Box 4340
Berkeley, Calif.
94704

Books by John-Raphael Staude:

Max Scheler. An Intellectual Portrait
The Adult Development of C.G.Jung

Edited Volumes:

Humanistic Society
Consciousness and Creativity
Wisdom and Age

Library of Congress Cataloging in Publication Data
Main entry under title:
Wisdom and Age

    "Book is the result of a conference and several seminars conducted by
Proteus Institute in Big Sur and the Wright Institute in Berkeley, Califor-
nia."
    Bibliography: p.
    1. Old age - Psychological aspects - Congresses. 2. Aged - Psychology
- Congresses. 3. Aging - Psychological aspects - Congresses. 4. Life cycle,
Human - Congresses. 5. Experience - Congresses. I. Staude, John-
Raphael.
HQ1061.W57   305.2'6   80-27744
ISBN 0-89496-111-X
ISBN 0-89496-110-1 (pbk.)

Table of Contents

Creativity and Community

Death and the Continutiy of Life

PREFACE

"Some sigh for yesterday. Some for tomorrow. But you must reach old age before you
can understand the meaning of the word
today."- Paul Claudel (at 80)

This book is the result of a series of symposia conducted
by Proteus Institute in Big Sur and the Wright Institute in
Berkeley, California. The symposia were supported in part
by a grant from the California Council for the Humanities.
The grant was given to encourage humanities scholars to
investigate and discuss public policy issues, such as aging.
The symposia and this book were designed to illuminate
the aging process as an adventure and an opportunity for
growth, something to be anticipated rather than to be
feared.

The title "Wisdom and Age" comes from the seminal
work of Erik Homberg Erikson. In his analysis of the life
cycle, Erikson postulates developmental tasks and possible
virtues to be acquired in each phase of the life cycle. In
mature adulthood, according to Erikson, the principle task
of adults is to establish and guide the next generation. The
life task is generativity vs. stagnation. The virtue is "care".
"If there is any responsibility in the cycle of life, it must be
that one generation owes to the next that strength by which
it can come to face ultimate concerns in its own way -
unmarred by debilitating poverty or by neurotic concerns
caused by emotional exploitation[1]."

In old age, according to Erikson, we face a struggle between arriving at a sense of integrity - that all in all our life has been worthwhile - or a sense of futility and despair. The virtue we can develop in old age is "wisdom," which Erikson defines as "detached concern with life itself in the face of death itself." "It maintains and conveys the integrity of experience, in spite of the decline in bodily and mental functions. It responds to the need of the oncoming generation for an integrated heritage and yet remains aware of the relativity of all knowledge[2]."

According to Erikson's theory, attaining wisdom indicates the completion and continuity of the life cycle. Wisdom is the product of a life fully lived. It indicates the time when the individual can see and accept his own life as coming to an end and when he can see and accept the cycle of his generation concluding itself as the next generation unfolds. The aging person must transfer his strength to the next generation so they in turn can face ultimate concerns in their own way. Although with increasing age there tends to be a decrease in potency, adaptability and performance, Erikson maintains that the strength of wisdom can balance the despair of these events.[3] "Only such integrity can balance the despair of the knowledge that a limited life is coming to a conscious conclusion, only such wholeness can transcend the petty disgust of feeling finished and passed by, and the despair of facing the period of relative helplessness which marks the end as it marked the beginning.[4]"

Erikson's provocative interpretation of the life cycle and his views on integrity and wisdom as the tasks of later life was the inspiration which inspired me to convene this symposium and each presenter's focus initiated the convening of the relationship between wisdom and age. The resultant papers raise a number of related questions. Are there any particular understandings that become more available to us as we grow older? If education continues throughout life, what kinds of learning are most appropriate for people after mid-life? in old age? Does the character of scientific or artistic work change as the creative person grows older? How does the aging process differ for men and women? What can we learn about successful aging from studying the lives of vital older people?

Although the papers gathered here were presented by scholars working within a variety of different disciplines and viewpoints, a few unifying themes reccur through the entire volume. One theme is that, as Dr. Weininger put it, "aging is a lifelong affair" and "life has no age". The definition of what constitutes old age is problematic. Is it determined biologically, psychologically, sociologically, culturally, or economically? We begin aging from the time we are born; growing old is a process that occurs throughout our lives. It seems as though old age is a function of the life we have lived.

Another theme that runs through many of these essays is the recognition that old age offers a unique opportunity for personal development on all levels; cognitive, moral, emotional, and particularly spiritual. The papers by Meeker and Halifax discuss development in the broader context of environmental and cross-cultural ethnological studies. Naranjo and Friedman examine the religious and philosophical aspects of adult development and aging[5]. Sanford and Simpson discuss the psychological and moral issues faced by older adults. The field of adult development and aging is as yet relatively undeveloped.[6] We hope that these papers will add a humanistic perspective to this emerging new field.

A third theme in this book is that aging is an opportunity for creative behavior of all kinds. None of us have been old before. We have to invent our own way of growing old and growing wise. Perhaps the example of other creative innovators before us can help inspire and guide us on our journey into the unknown. Richard Wiseman examines the late works of creative genius like Einstein, Beethoven, Rembrant, and performing artists like Rubenstein and Casals, to uncover some of the characteristics of creativity in later life. Downing and Friedman discuss the late works of Sophocles, Jung, Mann, Elliott, Yeats, and Buber in similar fashion. Throughout the entire volume one finds numerous references to Dante, the archetypal mid-life pilgrim[7] It is perhaps only natural that humanists, when called upon to reflect upon old age, should draw from their familiarity with the classics of literature and philosophy to illustrate the relationship between wisdom and age.[8]

Many of the writers who contributed to this volume would probably not be classified as elderly. Their average age is about 45. This brings us to another theme; concern with death. At mid-life we become aware of our finitude. No longer looking out on the open vistas of youth, our life begins to contract, and we become more reflective as we become increasingly aware of the inevitability of our own death. In our time, medical science and an improved standard of living have extended the life span. Is the concern with death that comes to many people at mid-life a carry-over from earlier times when most people died before age 45? Today, old age has become inextricably associated with death, as the end of the aging process. The way we treat dying and death affects our view of old age. The papers by Charles Garfield and Margaret Keys take up the issue of death most directly, but if, as Montaigne says, philosophy is a preparation for death, then one might recognize *that* stands as a shadow behind this whole book.[9]

I want to take this opportunity to acknowledge and thank everyone who helped make our symposia and this book a success. In particular I want to thank my dear mother, an eighty year old artist who has been an inspiration to many and who kindly donated the use of her Big Sur estate for the symposia. I also want to thank Dr. Ben Weininger whose presence as the wise old man at the symposium was invaluable. Lastly, I want to thank my editorial assistant and friend, Margaret Stetson, for her invaluable help.

FOOTNOTES

1. Erik H Erikson. *Insight and Responsibility* (New York; Norton, 1964) p.133.

2. Erik H. Erikson. *Idenity and the Life Cycle. Psychological Issues* Vol.1, No. 1(1959) p.98

3. For a penetrating critique of "Erikson's Theory of Human Development as it Applies to the AgedWisdom as Contradictive Cognition" see the article of this title by Vivian Clayton in *Human Development,* 18 (1975) pp. 119-128 and her article written with James E. Birren, "The Development of Wisdom across the Life Span: A Reexamination of an Ancient Topic," in *Life-Span Development and Behavior,* Vol. 3. New York: Academic Press, 1980 pp. 103-135.

4. Erikson. *Insight and Responisbility,* p. 134.

5. Compare Claudio Naranjo's essay "The Way Up and the Way Down: On Meditation". in *Consciousness and Creativity* (Berkeley; Ross Books, 1977), pp. 85-94.

6. For a discussion of the development of adult development and Jung's contributions to this emerging field see John-Raphael Staude. *The Adult Development of C.G.Jung* (London: Routledge and Kegan Paul, 1981)

7. See also Margaret Frings Keys, "Dante and the Tasks of Individuation, *"International Journal of Art Psychotherapy* Jan. 1978, pp.1-7.

8. Compare another volume of essays by humanists on *Aging, Death and the Compeletion of Being* edited by David D. Van Tassel (Philadelphis; University of Pennsylvania Press, 1979)

9. As a result of the interest in "death" in last year's symposium the theme of the 1981 Eranos-West Proteus Symposium is *Creativity and Death*. For more information or to order the forthcoming Volume 3 of *Proteus Papers* write John-Raphael Staude, Proteus Institute, Anderson Canyon Road, Big Sur, Calif., 93920.

The Wisdom of Experience

THE WISDOM OF EXPERIENCE

John-Raphael Staude

I believe that each season of life has its own particular character, value, and developmental tasks. We would not live as long as we do, if this longevity had no purpose or meaning for the species. The afternoon of life has just as much significance as life's morning and midday, but it is different. It is foolish to try to live out the afternoon of our lives according to the program developed in our childhood and youth. In my experience, mid-life is a time for re-evaluation and examination of the roads we have taken thus far, and the roads not taken. Very often for many people the later years provide opportunities to explore some of those roads not taken earlier.

With Carl Jung, I believe that the goal of each individual life is to become that unique person who we really are. This usually entails developing latent aspects of ourselves as we grow older. Those qualities we used to establish ourselves in the world when we were young may not be so useful or appropriate for us as in later life. As our life conditions change, we must adapt to them. On the other hand, although people do change a great deal as they grow older, deep within, they carry along with them certain clearly recognizable styles, traits, attitudes, and their essential character structure.

The wisdom of experience is latent within every one of us. It is called forth out of the depths of our own hearts as we make the shifts in values that the losses of later life often demand of us, as we move from concern with personal gratifications to the development of the self. The wisdom of experience, the sense of ripeness and satisfaction with one's life does not depend on those external sources which we so often use to bolster our self-esteem. Reputation, beauty, accomplishment, wealth, power, and influence—all these ephemeral qualities can never be securely achieved once and for all. Ultimately, all we really have to rely on is our selves, our own quality of being.

The major religious traditions of mankind have always rebelled against the identification of the person with his or her usefulness to society. In fact, the ultimate uselessness of all worldly things is a basic teaching of most religions. In Taoism, the most memorable celebration of uselessness occurs in the story Chuang Tzu told of a gnarled old tree. At first this tree attracted the eye of the woodsman. On closer examination, it seemed useless for his purposes. However, it was this very uselessness that guaranteed the tree its longevity when all the other more useful trees had been cut down. Again, in the Christian Gospels we are reminded that we are not saved through our own achievements, but through God's grace and bountiful love. In short, the religious traditions confirm the insight of modern psychology: that the basis of our self-worth is independent of economic productivity and social role. Retirement entails a change in social role and economic status; it should not result in a declining sense of self-esteem.

Of all life's realities, old age is one of the most difficult to imagine. What does it mean, to "get old"? When are we "old enough" to be "old"? There is no internal clock within us to tell us the exact time of our lives. We may feel old, yet be chronologically young. We may be over ninety years old, yet feel young.

To most of us old age and death are abstractions, hard to relate to, difficult to grasp, far away. We live as if we will never die. Yet for many of us it is easier to imagine being dead than being old. Death, after all, is usually conceptualized as a state of nonbeing, a void, but nevertheless a state in which people imagine they retain their identities. For people who believe in immortality, a persons' present identity either continues in death or changes according to how well his life was lived. On the other hand, being an old person means conceiving of oneself as a different person, a markedly changed being. Unlike death, old age means a physical and psychological mutation of the self forced upon is by the ravages of time and the decay of the body and the mind. So people tend to avoid conceiving of themselves as being "old." And they tend to avoid contact with old people almost as if age were a contagious disease.

In recent years the situation has begun to change. Innovative programs like SAGE and SHANTI have brought many people into direct or indirect contact with the realities of aging and dying. A stream of books and articles on aging has appeared and is growing. Television programs like "Over Easy" have brought our elders into our living rooms. The demystification of aging is continuing, but nevertheless many stereotypes still prevail. Take a moment, now, to examine your own attitudes, images, and feelings about being old. Visualize your body and your life when you are old. Pay particular attention to where your images of aging come from. Do you look forward to getting old? Do you dread it? What was it like for your parents or members of your family? How old do you expect to be when you die? Since we have no direct experience of being old we tend to get our images from what we observe old people around us are like.

The way older people see themselves and their needs is very different from what we might expect and what others predict. In research done by Bennet and Eckman[1], people of different ages were given sentences about older people to complete. Here are some examples:

1. In general, old people need _____
2. One of the greatest fears of many old people is_____
3. Old people tend to resent _____
4. One of the greatest pleasures of old people is _____

Think about your answers before reading further.

Some of the results of the survey were surprising. For example:

1. In general old people need _____
   Younger people most often named assistance as the major need of old people. Older people cited their dominant need as wanting to be liked and valued by others.

2. One of the greatest fears of many old people is _____
   Younger people said that death and dying were great fears. Older people most often stressed a lack of money and financial insecurity. Death is not actually the primary fear of old people. Their fears are more immediate, reflecting realistic insecurity in regard to the opportunities available.

3. Old people tend to resent _____
   Younger people thought that the old resent the young. In fact, the old said they most resented being rejected by others.

4. One of the greatest pleasures of old people is _____
   Younger people judged that the greatest pleasure was the family, while older people more frequently chose companionship and love.

Do peoples' attitudes grow more negative as they themselves age? Many individuals report that the older they get the happier they become. Even with regard to sex, they say it gets better and better. Unless they are in poor health, people rarely judge themselves as being old. "Old" usually refers to the way we see others. We think of "those old people" even when we are old chronologically. And how old "old" is changes for us as we get older. Being old seems always to be something in the future.

We may never be "old", but we are always aging, and this aging process forces us to deal with change. As we grow older our lives change. We face new unfamiliar tasks. Since we have never been old before in our lifetime, aging is an unending challenge and opportunity for creative behavior. Aging forces us to deal with the discontinuity of change.

Today it is a scandal the way we treat our old people. In earlier times and in other cultures the old person had an image of himself as an example and an important repository of the past, one whose life could be summed up and extracted to provide a model for the young, and whose knowledge (especially of sacred ritual and tradition) could be directly transmitted in ceremonies over which he presided. An old Balinese legend makes this point very well.[2]

> It is said that once upon a time the people of a remote mountain village used to sacrifice and eat their old men. A day came when there was not a single old man left, and the traditions were lost. They wanted to build a great house for the meetings of the assembly, but when they came to look at the tree trunks that had been cut for that purpose no one could tell the top from the bottom: if the timber were placed the wrong way up, it would set off a series of disasters. A young man said that if they promised never to eat the old men any more, he would be able to find a solution. They promised. He brought his grandfather,

whom he had hidden, and the old man
taught the community to tell top from
bottom.

It seems that by ostracizing our old, we,too, have lost the traditions which helped us understand our own lives and to tell top from bottom.

In early times age also conveyed a sense of power and wisdom derived from old persons having traversed so much of life and experience that no one else had. The Elders moved beyond the struggles of ordinary life. They were treated with respect and fear, as they were close to the mysterious borderland of death and therefore more knowledgeable about it. The Elders reflect the sequence of life over the entire course of the life cycle, the shift from nature to culture, and the transmutation of personal experience into cultural forms. Through oral tradition the Elders transmit these cultural forms which give meaning and context to life. The essay by Joan Halifax in this book illustrates this well.

In traditional cultures, the old and the very young were often allies and playmates, "exemplars of ultimate thresholds at the begining and end of existence."[3] They are mutually attracted, knowing that they - and not the busy generation between - are playfully wise.

Here and there in contemporary society the old are still seen (and see themselves) as exemplars of a fulfilled life and mediators of ultimate cultural traditions. More often, however, the old carry only the image of the tainted death mask. They are caught in a vicious circle. We reject them and isolate them because they remind us of death and undermine our fantasies of perpetual youth. In this way we leave them deprived of a life function. They become scapegoats for our own deepest fears of death. Not surprisingly, in this culture in which the old are so often victims of exploitation, they rarely manifest the wisdom of the Elders of simpler cultures. In an almost self-fulfilling syndrome, too often, the rejected old manifest such bitterness and withdrawl that they produce further rejection on the part of the rest of society. In short, because the old remind us of our own mortality, we seclude them rather than honoring them.[4]

Furthermore, the speed of cultural change, mobility of family life, and the overall flux of symbol systems and ideologies today are factors in the decline of old age as a respectable and respected stage in life. Just as we get rid of obsolete, worn out machines, and replace them with newer, younger, more efficient ones, so do we also with people. Instead of being an asset, age and experience is often a liability in our rapidly changing technological culture. As I said before, behind all this frantic movement lies our fear of death.

Death seems to be the goal and term of life. Our life entails growth and development, decay and sooner or later death. The way we have lived seems often to be reflected in how we die. One of the tasks of life, as we get older, is to become reconciled to our own deaths. Perhaps one of the reasons for gerontophobia is because being around old persons can be a painful reminder of our own inevitable aging and death.

Recent research on midlife indicates that one of the characteristics of midlife is a growing awareness of getting closer to death. There is often also a sense of despair over lost opportunities and over the gap between one's youthful hopes and dreams and the realities of one's actual life structure. "Inexorable images of separation from others and from the life process in general, of an unbreakable habit of violated integrity, and of the mind caught in static closure in relation to whatever external events are taking place around it are prominent features of this despair. Not only are life projects negated, but one has lost hope of ever rendering them or oneself vital."[5]

On the other hand there is also a special quality of life power available only to those seasoned by struggles of 4 or more decades. "That seasoning includes extensive cultivation of images and forms having to do with love and caring, with experienced parenthood, with teaching and mentorship, with work combinations and professional creativity, with responses to intellectual and artistic images around one, and above all, with humor and a sense of the absurd."[6]

The title *Wisdom and Age* came to me through the work of Erik Erikson who suggests in his paradigm of the human life cycle that *wisdom* is the virtue of old age. Under favorable personal and cultural conditions, he says, wisdom may emerge out of our struggle to develop a sense of integrity as against ending our lives with a sense of despair and disgust. Ego integrity, he says, "is the acceptance of one's one and only life cycle as something that had to be and that, by necessity, permitted of no substitutions." It entails a new and different appreciation of one's parents and ancestors and a feeling of comradship with the ordering ways of distant times and different pursuits. Although he may be aware of the relativity of various life styles, the possessor of integrity is ready to defend the dignity of his own life style for he knows that an individual life is the accidental coincidence of but one life cycle with but one segment of history; and that for him all human integrity stands or falls with the one style of integrity of which he partakes. The style of integrity developed by his culture thus becomes the patrimony of his soul, the seal of his moral paternity of himself. "Wisdom, Erikson says "is the *detached and yet active concern with life itself in the face of death itself.*"[7] It maintains and conveys the integrity of experience in spite of the disdain over human failing and the dread of ultimate nonbeing."

The lack or loss of this accrued ego integration is signified by *fear of death*: the one and only life cycle is not accepted as the ultimate of life. Despair expresses the feeling that the time is now short, too short, for the attempt to start another life and to try out alternate roads to integrity. This despair often becomes chronic, hovering around regret over lost opportunities and over the gap between one's early hopes and dreams and the realities of one's life structure. Not only are life projects negated, but one has lost hope of ever rendering them or oneself vital.

A sense of integrity, on the other hand, a feeling that one has drained the cup of life to the full, that one is seasoned by experience of a long, full life is the fruit of a life well lived. One finds this well expressed by Irene Claremont di Castillejo in her inspiring book, *Knowing Woman*.[8]

The fundamental truth to remember in thinking of woman, irrespective of the role she plays, is that her life's curve, unlike that of man, is not a slow rising to the zenith of power followed by a gradual decline in the later years. The curve of a woman's life span follows more nearly the pattern of the seasons. She almost literally blossoms in the spring, but the long summer which follows is a very slow ripening with nothing much in the woman herself to show for it. If she lives a traditional family pattern she will be giving all the sap which rose so abundantly earlier to nourish her offspring, materially, emotionally, and spiritually.

Then suddenly her children are all grown up, gone on their separate journeys, and she finds herself bereft. The apparent purpose of her life, for which she had strained every nerve, is snatched from her with the attainment of the goal. She feels stranded on the mud flats, while the river races by bearing away each new craft as it embarks, and she no part of the flowing waters. What then? What can happen then with another 30 or 40 years of life still to run and no one needing her? Even her husband has centered his life on his career and other interests while she was occupied with her growing family. Now even at best his need of her is not absorbing enough to assuage her aching emptiness.

What them? This is the crucial moment in the life of any wife and mother. It is then she may notice, almost by accident, that from where the early blossoms fell fruit is hanging almost ripe—fruit which has grown unheeded and is now ready and waiting to be picked. The autumn of a woman's life is far richer than the spring if only she becomes aware in time, and harvests the ripening fruit before it falls and rots and is trampled underfoot. The winter which follows is not barren if the harvest has been stored, and the withdrawal of sap is only a prelude to a new spring elsewhere.

If there is a particular wisdom that comes with age and experience, it seems to be a kind of detached objectivity about one's life. The wise old person seems to recognize that personal worth does not depend on one's usefulness or contributions to society. This realization that one is more than what he or she does is a necessity for peace of mind particularly in old age when one's physical faculties begin to decline and one must make way for the next generation.

FOOTNOTES

1. Bennet, R. & Eckman, J. *Attitudes Toward Aging; A critical Examination of Recent Literature & Implications for Future Research.* C. Eisdorfer & M. Lawton (editors). The Psychology of Adult Development & Aging. , Washington D.C., American Psychological Association 1973.

2. Nouwen, Henry and Gaffney, J.M. and Gaffney, Walter J.. *Aging - The Fulfillment of Life* Garden City, N.Y., Image Books, 1976

3. - 6. Lifton, Robert J. *Broken Connection: On Death & the Contunity of Life.* N.Y., Simon & Shuster 1979

7. Erickson, Erick H. *Childhood & Society* Norton, N.Y., 2nd edition 1963

8. De Castillejo, Irene Claremont. *Knowing Woman. A Feminine Psychology* N.Y., Harper & Row 1973

MEDITATION AND MATURITY:
IN GOD WE RUST

Claudio Naranjo

Even though spiritual development may ultimately lead to what we might call eternal life, it proceeds through a psychological death; and while in the end it may lead to rejuvenation, it can be argued that it leads to such rejuvenation through something akin to a premature aging. The dying away of a part of the personality that the spiritual guest involves can manifest, both subjectively and objectively, in signs that we associate with old age. Thus—"In God We Rust."

The ideas of death and resurrection or of falling to rise, are, as you probably know, at least as old as shamanism. In shamanism we find in the "higher religions" as statement of experience, the same motif that was to become religious dogma. Many shamans have reported to their inquisitive interviewers how, at the beginning of their career they underwent a living death, how, prompted by disease perhaps, they were taken to the underworld to be dismembered, or how their body was opened by spirits and the old organs removed, to be replaced by new ones. In these statements we can recognize essentially the same process that was articulated by the mysteries of antiquity—particularly by the Egyptian resurrection mysteries of Osiris, of which the Jewish teaching of the desert crossing toward the promised land, and the Christian mystery of resurrection are continuations.

In the Christian formulation you find the pattern broken down into stages: the Stations of the Cross may be taken not only at the literal level, but, as Thomas Aquinas affirms of scripture in general, as a reference to spiritual truth—and thus, in this case, to inner events in the course of a process of psychological dying on the way to the Great Rebirth. This understanding of the passion as each individual's "imitation of Christ" along the spiritual journey was generally accepted during the Middle Ages, as is reflected in the old saying that "few come to Bethlehem; fewer still come to Calvary." This idea of an internal death that we all undergo as we reach a certain stage of development is expressed in St. Paul's analogy of the "Old Man" and the "New Man": When the new man is born within us, he says, the old man receives a fatal blow. This is not his death, however, for the two men continue to live side by side within us for some time. As in the case of the Stations of the Cross, once more we find here a reference to a dying process that is not a once-for-all event, but which extends over a certain period of the inner journey. Dante, in his *Vita Nuova*, says that when he first saw Beatrice the animal spirit, "dwelling in that part where food is digested" began to weep and exclaimed, "Oh, wretched me! For I shall be distorted often from now on." Here too, we find the notion that spiritual fulfillment entails pain and loss to the "lower nature": the ordinary, worldly personality.

In her well-known book *Mysticism*, Evelyn Underhill, after surveying the lives of a number of Christian saints, arrives at a now well known generalization about the stages of their development: again and again she saw a pattern emerge in these lives: a stage of purification crowned by an illuminative stage (filled with visions, inspiration and ecstasy) which in turn recedes as the individual enters a stage where all spiritual progress seems lost, and which, in the fortunate cases, precedes the final state of union, the penultimate stage that St. John of the Cross called the "dark night of the soul" is characterized by an extinction of transcendental consciousness, an acute sense of imperfection, "spiritual ennui," intellectual impotence and loss of will power. It constitutes, in every visible way, a process of deterioration and so must society view it, for the condition tends to involve a loss of reputation. The experience of those who have crossed beyond this "valley of the shadow of death," however, reveals it as a time of ripening and purification. "Think not," says Tauler, "that God will be always caressing His children, or shine upon their heads, or kindle their hearts as He does at first. He does so only to lure us to Himself, as the falconer lures the falcon with its gay hood . . . We must stir up and rouse ourselves and be content to leave off learning, and no more enjoy feeling and warmth, and must now serve the Lord in strenuous industry and at our own cost."

One can say that old age imposes on us a measure of renunciation and the need to develop non-attachment, but anyone who is involved on the spiritual path imposes them on himself. In fact, if he comes as far as this "dark night," he finds that, for him too, life or the path imposes them. The path may be regarded as a speeding up of what will come to us anyhow. In it, renunciation is chosen as a way of life, as if to corner oneself—before time does—into the finding of another life, at least, it constitutes a concentration in learning from the difficulties of life. In Tibetan Buddhism, for example, coming to grips with the problems of ordinary living is regarded as the best preparation for spiritual development. It would seem that the frustrations of life can either be meaningless, or, if we embrace them in the attitude that Gurdjieff called "conscious suffering," an occasion for growth.

But not only does the spiritual path involve a speeding up of what comes to us naturally with organic deterioration; it can even lead to some symptoms and feelings of old age. I think that it is this experience that is reflected in fairy tales in what we call the Rip van Winkle motif. Typically, the hero travels to a magic land, beyond time (the illuminative stage of the journey) and when he returns he finds his city in ruins, and nobody that he knows is alive, for many generations have elapsed. Then he, too, suddenly ages and dies. This does not mean that he should have stayed in the magic land, but that is just as it is: the tale echoes a knowledge of that stage of the inward journey at which the individual returns to the world and becomes aware of a psychological aging and dying.

Also Odyseus looks like an old man when he returns to Ithaca—even though Homer tells us that Pallas Athena only disguises him thus. His ships have all been sunk, his men are dead—his journey of return after the conquest of Troy and the liberation of Helen is, again, the dark night of the Soul. He is weary of what seems an interminable journey, yearns to be home, and finally arrives, as an old beggar— the penultimate stage. And in Faust, the motif of falling to rise is taken to the extreme. When he dies, and Mephistopheles is about to take his soul, at the end, it is snatched away from him, and Faust is saved. Goethe has been criticized for this *deus et machina* in the last scene, but I think that it reflects the deepest wisdom: perhaps only when you think that you are lost, you can be saved. You have to go to the very end.

Among the allegories of the spiritual journey, however, it is Al-Ghazzali's Minhaj Al-Abidin (The Way of the Submitted) that best conveys the theme that I am pursuing—viz: that of spiritual development as premature aging. Like Attar had done before him in his "Parliament of Birds," Al-Gazzali (ref: *The Elephant in the Dark,* by Idris Shah in book of same title. L. Lewin, ed.) writing in the eleventh century, speaks of seven valleys that need to be crossed along the mystical path. Only the first, the Valley of

Knowledge, is outwardly positive, and from there on the way is down, much as in the stations of the cross. The second is called the Valley of Repentance, and we may conjecture that it corresponds to the process of life-review that sets in spontaneously with the ripening of age. It is followed by the Valley of Stumbling Blocks, where he will have to face four psychological troubles: anxious care about survival, as a result of his retirement; doubts and anxieties about his private affairs; worries, hardships and indignities for want of social contact (for when man wishes to serve God, Satan attacks him), and unpleasant happenings and unexpected sufferings as the outcome of his destiny. Does not all this resemble the problems of old age? From here the poor worshipper proceeds to the Valley of Tribulations, where he is enjoined to be patient in sufferings and joyous in submission to God's will; then to the Thundering Valley and the Abyssmal Valley—before he may come to the Valley of Hymns, "Where, mortal as he was, he tried his best to sing the songs of promise to the Immortal Being."

The overall pattern of the process is that of a spiritual honeymoon (comparable to Underhill's "Illuminative" stage) followed by a descent to the point where, by a kind of turning around of perspective, you find yourself at the top. This constitutes, more than a falling to rise, a falling which in itself has been all along a rising in disguise, or a single process of falling-rising, of which only one aspect is obvious until the end. This aspect of the common human odyssey is conveyed by Dante when he describes the journey from the dark forest to Earthly Paradise as a straight line passing through the center of the earth: up to this point, it is a descent into hell; after that, a rising toward the top of Mount Purgatory. The same observation about the pattern of the process of spiritualization recurs in the work of a contemporary Chilean poet that I have recently translated into English. David Rosemann's "The Sky is the Fountain" consists of a series of twenty "stations" that correspond to experiences between death (which occurs in the book's first verse) and what has traditionally been called the Kingdom, and in this book is "el prado" . . . the meadow. The sky in the poem is life, and the fountain, a world of reflections or echoes, an intermediate stage that the soul must cross on its way to a condition which is neither life nor death, and yet both. The outer story is that of a fifteen-year old girl—Jesusa, throughout the twenty stations that comprise the poem, goes deeper and deeper into the fountain; until she reaches "the dome-most dome" at its bottom: in the world of reflection, the lowest is the highest. Then she rends her heart; she nails it down and proceeds without identity. She has become nothing, and can thus proceed to the meadow (the "prado") —which "delivers what you asked for most". As in Al-Ghazzali's work, the pattern of the journey in this contemporary poem is down and down to the highest. It contains a rich phenomenology of the "dark night of the soul." A recurrent idea in it is that of a growth that is sustained by deterioration, a regeneration nourished by rotting, a self-construction which is the less apparent aspect (until the end) of self-destruction.

If the process of spiritualization, as so consistently described, feeds on the sacrifice of body and worldly mind, if it parallels the natural process of aging unto death— leading, indeed, to a sort of death before dying—a corollary naturally suggests itself: is not aging, then, the outer aspect and basis of our nature-given spiritual evolution, our built-in preparation for death and our schooling in transcendence?

Something of this is, I assume, implicit in the title of this symposium: The Age of Wisdom. And perhaps all of us know individuals who indeed became naturally wise as they approached their end: more discriminating between the substantial and the ephemeral, less concerned with their self-image, less fearful—in sum, less dominated by what traditional Asian psychologies call the ego, the little mind. I have had occasion to witness it in my mother, who in some sense started living after sixty, and even in an aging genius, Totila Albert, who was among those few that came to Calvary—and to spiritual rebirth in the middle of his life. He was well known in Chile as a sculptor, though his more important and vast poetical work in German remains unknown. At the age of 72 he had a brain stroke, and his bio-computer started failing—yet I had with him some of the deepest conversations at this time when his arithmetic was at its worse. I once asked him whether he was glad that he had survived. As I have said, he was one of those who, much earlier in life, had "died before dying," and more than once I had heard him say in his old age (but before the stroke) "What am I doing, hanging around in this old corpse? I have already done my job." But this time, he said, "I would not have wanted to miss these years. Life is an evolution of consciousness, and consciousness grows and grows."

In other cases, we also know, old age seems but a calamity. But doesn't the spiritual pain itself seem a calamity when we are in the middle of its "dark night"?

If the process triggered by psycho-spiritual technologies is similar to what the natural one can potentially *be*, does this not suggest that the shape of the process - a falling to rise, or a falling towards the highest - is also similar, and that perhaps we can even recognize the same stages?

The corollary of this is one that the Hindus applied many centuries ago—in prescribing for old age no other responsibility than that of the sanyasin, the renunciate who turns his attention completely toward the transcendent. Applied today, this view of aging would imply, among other things, that centers for the care of the aged become, in some measure, spiritual schools.

Interview between John-Raphael Staude and Claudio Naranjo:

JRS: I'd like to ask you this personally: having written the paper, how does it relate to your own life?

CN: That is a very pertinent question, for when you asked me to take part in the symposium my first reaction was to decline on the grounds of my scant experience with old age. Then, when you insisted, I asked myself: well, what do I know from experience? And I became aware that there was a single idea that I felt motivated to talk about, and that this—the idea of spiritual development as premature aging—was suggested by a recent stage of my own life process.

Even though I am now rejuvenating, it is only during this year, or perhaps the one before, that I have felt my aging in a keen sense. Suddenly I was not in the young generation any more. It is curious how the sense of being a kid persisted in my life past the mid-forties, and I haven't completely lost it; though I am finally beginning to feel really grown up, and even ancient at times—in the face of youthful illusions and ambitions. But before coming to this incipient ripeness I become aware of physical deterioration and other symptoms of old age. It would seem that I had to undergo a period of senility before coming to true adulthood. First my body outline changed, and before I even knew that I was not skinny any more I had grown a considerable belly; then, one day, I realized that I could no longer run around the block without great strain. This happened at a time of being very sedentary while immersed in a contemplative striving of diminishing returns. This came after a high plateau, a period of blossoming, during which I was very active and extroverted. As the sense of spiritual abundance that was past of it receded I both sought to recover it through spiritual practices and lost incentive to help others in the same direction—which was my work.

I became very introverted, uninterested in social contact, in speaking or writing, even in reading. In an outer sense I was quite unproductive, and even my life of meditation was becoming less and less productive—in the sense of having "high" experiences or profound ones—even though I felt that I was always making progress in some sense, and in retrospect I see that I went through a purification. A "purification through putrefication" once said my friend Leon Lurie, a Washington psychoanalyst. For in any visible sense things were negative: loss of grace, loss of energy, of joy, of motivation, of achievement, of contact with people—even of money: for how can an isolated "old man" like that survive?

JRS: Didn't you also have a physical illness?

CN: That's true, true. I had a long illness, in fact, which was not clearly diagnosed, and probably went on for quite a while before I knew it - which was partly the cause of the heaviness I felt. I not only consulted with regular physicians about it, but also some healers—for I didn't relish the prospect of surgery—and they independently agreed in seeing the illness as the con-commitant of a spiritual crisis. agree:

I never felt tragic, but, imperceptively, in an attempt to cultivate equanimity, I had lost the wish to live

I clearly remember being confronted with the question, "Do I want to live?" I couldn't give a whole-hearted answer—I honestly couldn't. More than one friend said, "Why don't you pray?" But I truly didn't want to do that. "How do I know what is God's will?" was my reaction.

JRS: Did you ever have a sense of wanting to die?

CN: No.

JRS: You didn't have to make a decision, you didn't have to make a choice of whether you would kill yourself?

CN: It was a kind of withdrawal from life, which I think had something to do with my meditation process; a detachment before the emergence of something new.

JRS: How did it happen that something new emerged for you?

CN: I felt it coming in my creative work—a joy of discovering, a very subtle happiness that comes from understanding things in a new way. Incipiently, too, a new level of competence—I see this coming in my writing, for instance. It is not that I feel very drawn to write—though the impulse is growing. Perhaps I would not be doing it unless people asked my to write ...

JRS: Why do you write?

CN: I have a motto: "eat what falls dead at your feet"—I take circumstances as indicators of destiny. So when you asked me to talk, for instance, I felt that it was right to respond to that. I want to be useful, to pay my dues in this life, and the most specific thing that I have to offer is my experience and understanding. I had become adjusted to doing nothing, or doing a minimum, but there is a kind of satisfaction that comes only from inspired creativity and from accomplishing something.

JRS: You do feel that you want to make a difference after all?—Not just to withdraw into meditation?

CN: Yes, I feel that I went on a long pilgrimage, and now—

JRS: I am reminded of Plato's allegory of the cave and other images of withdrawal and of return. The withdrawl, of going down, the making of the journey, and then at the end, in some way, the return to the world.

CN: Yes.

JRS: How are you coming back to the world, yourself, back to your life?

CN: In a number of ways. It interests me to see that I am coming to my very first serious interests. I mentioned the translation of Rosemann's book. I was keenly interested in his poetry as a teenager. It was an important part of my growing up to absorb the vision of life very cryptically expressed in his poetry. Then this interest was for a long, long time postponed. I also mentioned Totila Albert, another poet, one of the strongest influences in my youth. I am also coming now to a time when I begin to feel ready to come back to his work and editing it for publication. I think especially of his enormous epic, five volumes of one hundred and twenty cantos each. German is not my native language, so this is a big enterprise for which I have not felt ready, though now I am at the verge of readiness.

I was very interested during the years of my medical training in the issue of psychological types. I studied psychiatry with Matte Blanco at the University of Chile who was enthusiastic about the ideas of Sheldon, and I became very enthusiastic too. Then I became a student of psychoanalysis, and worked with Cattell who did the most thorough factor analytic studies of personality. I studied Eysenk too, and worked with characterology. Now I find myself beginning to write a book on characterological types, reflecting my many involvements, and bringing to it a lot of experience.

JRS: Yes. Do you have other writing projects going? Besides the one on the psychological types?

CN: I have two books under way—one is on types, and another on, (ah), myself. It's a very slow growing book which I started when I thought I just could do it in my spare time. My motivation then was to use an autobiographical thread to piece together ideas about many things. As time has gone on, I have found myself not available to work on it. I find that it is *not* something I can do at odd moments, but which requires much concentration, and am only working on it about one month per year. Last year I worked for three weeks in Sweden during a stay in a friend's house where I was very isolated, and had no interruptions. It has been growing about one chapter a year.

JRS: Has the subject changed in the course of time?

CN: No, but my conception is different. I don't feel like writing about ideas so much, as I had originally intended, but instead, I am interested only in the story-telling part of it. The beads have disappeared and only the thread is left.

JRS: What were the types of ideas you wanted to write about?

CN: Being a story of my pilgrimage, it would naturally go into the idea of various teachings. I am calling the second chapter of my book, "Meetings with Remarkable Men." But I am now talking more about myself than I had foreseen, and enjoying it increasingly. Even though I have not written so much, I see coming together within me the connection between the events in my experience, the natural artistry of life, a coherence that we don't create, but that is there for us to discover. So, as of today, I see the book as being more a work of art than any I wrote before, and this is something which could be of an interest beyond its explicit content.

JRS: So you are enjoying the craft of writing—

CN: Yes, I'm enjoying that—that's new in my life.

JRS: I know you have composed music, and you have played the piano; have you ever thought of writing fiction?

CN: Ah, no, except for a few short stories I wrote in my teens. But this autobiography in some sense will have some qualities of fiction, without being fiction, in that it involves the art of the story teller.

JRS: In your autobiography—are you still thinking of that image of up and down the holy mountain?

CN: When I called the book *Up and Down the Holy Mountain*, I envisioned dealing with a very specific segment of my life, the Arica experience, and its aftermath. It involved, specifically, my having been sent to the desert with intense motivation and well equipped with spiritual technology at a very special time in my life, the account of a great explosion that followed, and what I did with it. But as of today, I am not so enthusiastic about telling "what I did with it," for what once seemed to be the fruit of my life now seems to me to have been an apprenticeship—a teaching apprenticeship. Of course there is a chapter on that, and then another called "The Black Hole" with which I expect to end, even though I look upon the "Dark Night" as one who has mostly left it behind.

JRS: When you started the book, it was not yet winter, it was only autumn.

CN: It was the end of the fall, and so I still felt the enthusiasm of being retrospective—With the winter perspective, it became more interesting to write about my whole life, not just about the episode that prompted me in the first place. Yet this was a time of incubation rather than waiting.

JRS: If you will excuse me for saying so, it seems very much like a rather typical mid-life crisis situation - would you say that this was how you would describe your experience?

CN: I think that might be said.

JRS: In what way is it different?

CN: In the first place, I understand that the typical mid-life crisis is one where the person comes to saturation with the pursuit of the goals of life as it has been lived until then. The adolescent dream has been realized, the person has basically "made it." Then the journey turns inward, as Jung puts it, and the process of individuation becomes paramount. It is the time of starting the pilgrimage. For me that started earlier, and I had even come to the "Holy Mountain" of the pilgrimage, the great epiphany, before the endarkment. I see this as what mysticism has called, after St. John of the Cross' term for it, the "dark night of the soul. It has the same structure as the mid-life crisis or good-bye to the "first half of life": the quest has been fulfilled—the Grail has been seen—and there comes both a spiritual saturation and a renunciation of sustaining the spiritual longing and striving that has been visionary experience. Altered states of consciousness are lost, and this is perceived as spiritual dryness into a fall from the blessing, but is actually a hidden renunciation and a stabilization of consciousness. It is the beginning of wisdom but seems dark in the same way that the mole (according to Aesop) that looks to the light at the end of his tunnel, thinking he has been blinded, feels that he has come from day to night.

I imagine that this second life-crisis may be destined to occur naturally at an age, intermediate between the mid-life proper and the onset of old age, though disciplined and skillfully-guided spiritual practice can speed up the process.

I might just as well share with you my intuition of the life passages:

First you have childhood and then puberty, at around 12, a first step toward autonomy, a first degree of awakening and liberation.

Then, at the time when the femur's ossification is completed and thus our body comes to the completion of growth, at about age 24, the young adult emerges. You become autonomous, to a higher degree, achieve a second level of liberation from dependency on parents and environment.

Then comes the age that Dante speaks of as "The Middle of the Way of Life." To continue with 12-year cycles, let us say, 36, even though he said 35. Young bloomers like Keats and Schubert end their lives by this time, but average bloomers start their higher life.

Then comes around the age of 48, the age that I am talking about—the time of the end of questing—which is definitely not the end of growing and learning. It is a time of returning, of coming home after the quest, to the world with a measure of wisdom, a time of sowing.

Old age proper, starting around 60, is, I think, a mature school of renunciation that serves to bring to a higher perfection the mind of one who is prepared enough to cope with the experience.

I think that the reality of human life is that very few human beings come to wisdom—that is, gnosis—and even fewer reach maturity. Indeed, a high proportion of the population is forever stuck, unknowingly, in an abortive puberty crisis, and never fully leaves childhood behind.

I think that our life is designed in such a way that to each biological age corresponds a certain potential experience, but that to effect a passage we need to have completed the previous passage. If we are not mature for a crisis, then, we are likely to fail that crossing too. Not having completed "making it" in the world of work and relationship, for instance, will be detrimental to the spiritual path: and if the spiritual path as first fruit is retarded, the individual may be stuck on being an immature thirsty seeker and never come to wisdom and compassion. It would be natural to think that even fewer are ready for this stage of life than for the preceeding one, and, to continue the progression, fewer still are ready, by the time of old age, to enter the final purgatory and school for death.

So, to return to your question as to whether my "dark night" might be a mid-life crisis: I think that we may have to distinguish between an early and a late mid-life crisis, a time of taking off and a time of returning.

In my experience, the process involved a way up and a way down, an exalted state and then a swing of the pendulum in the opposite direction—an explosion and implosion, and now I feel that I am coming to a balance of "day and night" and a measure of detachment from both.

JRS: My first question to you was, "What in your own experience leads you to think about these things?" You told me about your life experience now, and in a lot of ways it parallels what you talked about as the aging process.

CN: Yes. An aging before aging—At least as related aging to the midlife crisis. I think the reason why my initial response was to relate my process to the ideas that I presented in the paper, that is to the night of the soul rather than to the mid-life crisis—was that to me—the depressive stage was so intimately connected to the stage of excitement—it was almost as a matter of consequence. A period of deflation after one of inflation—The inflation that followed upon the spiritual breakthrough led me to the point of seeing through my narcissism, and I suspect that this is a general process. Let's say that the neurotic side of our "normal" personality is rooted always in a truly crazy unconscious core ... I think that any radical transformation involves the transformation of that core, and that is very difficult unless it is lived out. That living out for me was a kind of subtle craziness. It was Messianic inflation ... I was very much appreciated as Messianic gurus usually are; I was at the pinnacle of my popularity; I had a great following, etc.; I was not usually regarded as crazy; I did very good work and if I look retrospectively, I see that I was useful, yet ...

JRS: You had a spiritual school then, "The Seekers After Truth"?

CN: Yes, Seekers After Truth, but still I was grandiose, and I was living out what had been my latent grandiosity, till then buried under a shy temperament and a tendency to put myself down. Only when I felt completely fulfilled and totally sure of myself because I had a "straight line to heaven," was I able to live my grandiosity. When I did that, and I could see it for what it was, it started breaking apart by itself. So, when I talk about psychological dying in my case, this started, it was ignited, by the flame of psychological inflation, a flame which in itself was ignited by a spiritual awakening that stirred me not only spiritually, but in my ego.

JRS: I am reminded of a phrase of Jung's. I don't know the exact words, but "He who approaches God, approaches the fire, must do so with caution," something of that sort. I think of Nietzsche as you describe—and Nietzsche's identification with Zarathustra, and the sort of manic personality inflation that he went through and unfortunately he never quite came down from that afterward. What's valuable in your experience if you write about it in your autobiography is to describe the way down. Because that is the only way we know. It is sort of like the Icarus complex. We know that the man flies high and then we see the crash. We don't really have a knowledge of the process, or of the natural completion of that process.

CN: As it became more obvious that it was winter season, I lost the motivation to write. It is not quite motivating to write the story of one's life when one's tree is not in full bloom. I have not fully uncovered it, in spite of the emerging excitement.

CN: Yes. Unfortunately, I did not keep journals during those years. I have journals of my life up to the point of the way down; then I lost all motivation to record my experience.

JRS: Perhaps it's just as well that you didn't keep a journal. Maybe it was necessary behaviorally to let go of attachment to knowing what was happening.

CN: It was not hard to let go. I lost my interest.

JRS: But it strikes me that the last time I talked to you, you mentioned that you have a tendency to accept a writing assignment such as this one we just completed in a way to jog you up so that you will do something. If you don't accept a few obligations, you are afraid that you'll do nothing, is that true? Or not so much any more?

CN: No, I'm not afraid I'll do nothing. My experience is that I am always doing something. And even during those relatively unproductive years, I always trusted that this fallow period was a temporary and needed regression.

JRS: And now you are going off to Chile?

CN: Yes. Last year I made an annotated translation of Rosemann's "The Sky and the Fountain," Now I will go to get the author's feedback and proceed to a revision.

JRS: Your main work, now, is your writing. You're not doing therapy any more?

CN: No, I have not wanted to take on clients because I would then delay this trip and writing, and I want to close this cycle. I do some teaching, at the California Institute of Integral Studies and at Nyingma Institute.

JRS: How old are you now?

CN: I will be 49 this November.

JRS: Forty-nine, that is a cabalistic number: 7 x7—

CN: Yes—this may be the year for me—the Year of the Monkey.

(laughter)

[end of interview]

SAGE AND WISDOM

by Gay Gaer Luce

This book conveys the richness that age and wisdom connote. The disciplines and approaches of the contributors to this volume are quite diverse, reflecting the fact that there is no one proper way to grow old any more than there is a single form of wisdom. Perhaps each of us is a hologram, an infinitesimal part of the Hologram. Wisdom seems to include an awareness of the larger whole that is the real context of our lives. Several of the essays in this book explore the ways in which the experience of life can open us to a deepening awareness of the interconnectedness of all things.

To me, wisdom has something to do with the melting of boundries and concepts. Each of us comes into this world with distinctive physical, mental, and spiritual tendenciss. We each live out a unique personal history and see the world through the special lenses of our personality. From infancy on, of course, we are aging. To a greater or lesser extent, during this life process, we are aware that great light, great unity, great love and magnitude lie within us.

A part of wisdom may be remembering what we lose in the social training of childhood. In adulthood our lives become focused on the rules of man-made societies. Within the exigencies and deversions of our social life, many of us become distracted from our natural heritage, our roots. We forget our oneness with each other and the natural universe. We may glimpse those dimensions of our being in the night surges of our dreams, while making love, in moments of compassion or extreme stress, or while fixing tea or walking the dog. But for most of us this fundamental reality is not the living center of our conscious lives.

Is it necessary to be old to be wise, to be tempered by this greater reality to see in perspective the endless procession of trivia and self-importance that we can become engrossed in? Not necessarily. People of any age can tap into this wisdom. Take the example of young Ramana Maharshi, who as a teenager laid down on the floor of his family's house and saw the bubble of his individuality burst. Jesus, also, was a very young man whan he reached wisdom.

Perhaps, along with the many other glimpses we have forgotten because of our social habits and our obeisance to clock-time, we have also forgotten that time, as we experience it, has holes like Swiss Cheese through which we can experience timeless dimensions, simultaneous events, coextensive with the clock. Chronology is merely a point of view, one that has us entering a narrow and difficult situation during one lifetime. Perhaps we feel a bit squeezed and compressed by being limited to a single lifetime. Yet human form is an opportunity to be grateful for. After all, we could have been born lice or lizards. Human beings have much greater potential for expanding their awareness, so we may as well seize the opportunity to develop our consciousness as much as possible during this lifespan. By so doing, we can appreciate a dimension of being well beyond the confines of our limited personal lives and our social milieu. We can escape through the cracks in our clock-time to dimensions for which no clocks and no age are of much importance.

To expand awareness it seems we must let go of some of our boundaries, expectations, defenses, and our imagined separateness. This means giving up images and attachments that we have conceived to be our "selves". I know that this is not easy. No matter how I long to free myself from the cage of my ego-centeredness, I find breaking down the bars frightening, like a voluntary dying. Today many young people are attempting to do this by choosing a spiritual discipline or using tools of psychology. If we don't volunteer to enter a "wisdom school" , life itself may do the teaching. Lessons of self knowledge learned very late in life may be painful and I believe that some of the pain of illness is the self confrontation that happens when we are forced to stop distracting ourselves with busyness, and be still. We are so applauded for being busy and "productive" that many people even in their late seventies and eighties feel guilty about giving in to stillness. Without taking that time for interior work, and without the support to go about it in silence and feeling, it is hard to make room for inner change.

In 1974, when a group of us began the exploration that became SAGE - a senior actualization group - there were almost no nurturing environments for people over sixty in which self development was the focus. Ironically, there was much more available for people of college age. I had originally planned a growth program for children, thinking I wanted to offer kids those experiences and skills that would have made my own life freer, less fearful, and more hearty. I shifted my interest from kids of seven to people of seventy because I saw my mother transforming as she did some simple practices. Age no longer seemed like the relevant factor. It seemed that older people required the same kind of environment as young ones if they were going to plunge into deep interior learning, with a change in self image and a loosening of fixed views of the world. Older people, like young ones, needed challenge, the expectation of changing, permission to be natural, to play, to try out new stances without ridicule, and direct nurturance. SAGE was an attempt to provide such an accepting and supportive environment for older people who were willing to take the risk.

These were our starting premises, which seemed very "far out" back in 1974:

STARTING PREMISES: [1]

There is a purpose to old age: a future to be fulfilled. "The first part of life is for learning, the second for service, and the last is time for oneself." It is a time to discover inner riches, for self-development and spiritual growth. It is also a time of transition and preparation for dying, which is at least as important as preparation for a career or a family. Out of this inner growth come our sages, healers, prophets, and models for the generations to follow.

People need special conditions for deep growth: affirmation, challenge, guidance, stimulation, encouragement, support, deep emotional nourishment, and permission to be unselfconscious - to be themselves. These conditions are as necessary for older people as for children.

Growth and well-being are enhanced by increasing pleasurable experience. Rather than dwelling on problems and negative feelings, older people need to experience magnificent alternative ways of being, new facets of themselves, new ways of exploring and controlling their minds and bodies so that old problems recede and d ssolve.

Each person is unique and will unfold in his or her own way. A smorgasbord of techniques should be available so that each person can choose the ones that suit him or her best.

Nobody can be compared with anyone else. Each person's odyssey of development will be different, and so each person must be listened to carefully and supported through his or her particular needs and quirks, until the person finds his or her best way of unfolding.

Older people may develop faster than young people in certain respects. Older people already have experienced wisdom that young people need to read in books. They also have less investment in ego, since thay are no longer creating a career or raising a family, and this may give them the freedom to adopt new attitudes and life-styles.

Many of the ailments of age are reversible. Many chronic symptoms are the result of long-term reactions to stress, along with generally poor diet and sedentary life. After learning relaxation methods to "unstress", many symptoms diminish, and a person can regain vitality.

Our thoughts and attitudes create our feelings and shape our bodies and lives. Although we shape much of what we experience in life, we do not discover this source of control and creativity until we are well along in life and have learned millions of beliefs and habits that are not even conscious such as the way we sit down in a chair or respond when somebody uses language we don't like...Growth is the process of making these hidden components of ourselves conscious.

Old age can be a time of emancipation from the inhibitions and habits learned in childhood. From our early family life all of us absorbed social amenities such as being nice or putting up with boring situations or stern moral judgements on the "other" half of the world. This can be a time of emancipation from these constricting social customs and views.

Old age can be a time of truth. All things are transitory - human relationships, nations, the stock market, and life itself. Even the sun and stars are in transition. To grow old is to enter a major transition: The closer we come to death the closer we come to reality and truth. Usually we are forbidden to talk about this, although *it is the human condition.* The more openly we can share this transition, the more we can accept the greater reality that is our lives.

We wanted to offer a smorgasbord of methods for our groups of highly individuated people, and encourage each person to follow the path that seemed most appropriate. These initial volunteers were gutsy and highly motivated. Some of them had chronic symptoms of illness, depression, and a sense of isolation and futility. The SAGE program was not a form of therapy, however. We tried to generate positive alternative experiences, an atmosphere of communion and acceptance for each person to unfold as he or she needed. We tried to be purely elicitive, not expecting or setting out goals to be achieved. I still find this unconditional attitude of reeceptivity the hardest to maintain.

Because we evolved a form of shared leadership at SAGE, it was impossible for one point of view to become doctrine. By returning frequently to a state of communion in which personal judgements are irrelevant, and in which we regain acceptance of ourselves as we are, the process remains mostly elicitive.

It is seven years since we began our experiment. We have now seen healthy people, very sick people, people in nursing homes and residences. It is clear that people in their later years can unfold, whatever their circumstances, and that there is a unique reward in store for them when they do.

After many groups , traning programs, and workshops, SAGE began to spread. We began to notice that younger and younger people wanted to join groups that we thought were designed for the old. Perhaps this is because SAGE offers an ongoing and safe context for personal growth. Age separation seems artificial, and yet it has been rewarding to conduct relatively homogenous groups for older people. If everyone is near seventy then there is less tendency to make invidious comparisons during physical movements and exercises such as Yoga, less competitiveness and impulse to perform. Moreover, these homogenous groups have had richly satisfying discussions that may only be possible with age peers who have had some commonality of life experience. In the instance of SAGE, this has meant facing some of the realities of physical illness, of loss and grief, the personal meaning of dying, and many other topics that are not dinner table conversation among most friends.

Intergenerational contact is also important. As one young instructor commented about his reasons for staying with SAGE, "By being with older people I have learned a lot about what is of real value in life. I could never have learned this from my peers." This seems so natural - learning from elders - that it seems a little peculiar to maintain age barriers at SAGE, barriers which prevent younger people in search of unfoldment from receiving the richness of life experience and wisdom they can get from elders on the same path.

If our experience in this short time in our relatively tiny organization is any indication of what could happen among older (and younger) people when given the opportunity to grow, it ought to reverse the stereotypes about aging, and release into our society an intensity, wisdom, and creative leadership from a group of people we cannot afford to ignore. There isn't anyone else around who can give us the pertinent road maps of life itself.

FOOTNOTES

1. Gay Gaer Luce. *Your Second Life*. Vitality and Growth in Maturity and Later Years From the Experiences of the Sage Program. N.Y., Delacorte Press/Seymour Lawrence, 1976, pp. 7-8.

SHAMANISM AND AGING

Joan Halifax

For the Shaman, the world is alive. The universe is animate. Behind the world of appearances there is life energy force. The Shaman realizes that life is power. His task is to master that power, though it is invisible to the naive eye.

The Shaman is able to control the unseen. All phenomena in the universe are endowed with human qualitities, and are viewed as being subject to influence by the Shaman. In a cosmos that is essentially as unpredictable as the human realm, tapping into power allows for the possible reversal of death, transformation of form, and transcendence of space and time.

The initial call to power takes the Shaman into the realm of chaos, where the cosmos is disorderly, where power is freely transformed. As one Shaman said: "All that exists lives—the land walks around, the walls of the houses have voices of their own. Even the chamber vessel has its own separate land and house. Even the dead walk around and visit the living at night."[1]

The Shaman is able to go far beyond the normal boundaries of human action and interaction. The call to power can be very disorienting. The beginning of mastery can be ecstatic. The act of mastery implies that balance, equilibrium, has been achieved. Only after time and experience is the manifestation of untransformed power not potentially damaging. This is why the ordeals the Shamans must endure in their apprenticeship are so demanding. The abuse of power is all too common. Obstacles to power and knowedge are great. The hardship of learning functions to eliminate the least virtuous and strengthens the less virtuous.

The realization of power comes to us frequently in the midst of an ordeal, or crisis involving encounter with death. It comes suddenly, in an instant. The initiations of Shamans and the awakening of Kundalini and Zen masters to Enlightenment seem similar in tone. The entrance to the other world is accomplished in an action of total disruption of the taken for granted world. The way out of this chaos is found when fear has been overcome through surrender and its complement, mastery.

With the Shaman, mastery can take the metaphorical form of the battle between Shaman and spirits. The spirits adversaries become tutors as the Shaman learns the ways of the spirits who ravage and decay. In this way the neophyte learns the battlefield he or she must enter on behalf of others in the future. Here direct knowledge is acquired through experience. Out of this can come compassion and empathy. An elder from San Juan Pueblos put it thus: "What I am trying to say is hard to tell and hard to understand ...unless...you have been yourself at the edge of the Deep Canyon and have comeback unharmed. Maybe it all depends on something within yourself - whether you are trying to see the Watersnake or the sacred Corn Flower. Whether you go out to meet death to Seek Life. It is like this: as long as you stay within the realm of the great Cloud Beings, you may indeed walk at the very edge of the Deep Canyon and not be harmed. You will be protected by the rainbow and by the great Ones. You will have no reason to worry and no reason to be sad. You may fight the witches, and if you can meet them with a heart which does not tremble, the fight will make you stronger. It will help you to attain your goal in life; it will give you strength to help others, to be loved and liked, and to seek life."[2]

The Huichol shaman, Ramon Medina Silva, explained to anthropologist Peter Furst that the life energy force or *kupuri* of a deceased elder was the only soul capable of returning to the world of the living. The Huichols believe that five years after one has died, the soul of the deceased can rejoin the living in the form of a rock crystal. In this crystalized state, the soul is called *tewari*, meaning grandfather or ancestor. Ramon insisted that not all souls are capable of manifesting as rock crystals. He said, "Only the souls who were sixty, seventy years old, the old people, those with wisdom, come back. Not those who died at twenty-five or at thirty, those not. Because they are not yet complete, they are not wise, they are not *mara'akate* (shamans) or other wise people. They do not have the complete years; they died incomplete. Those more than fifty, those, yes. They have experience, wisdom, knowledge. Those come back after five years. Men that are sturdy, that have learned well, that have taken heed, with much energy and much strength, their thoughts filled with much wisdom. And the same for women, women who are wise, who have gone for the peyote, who have knowledge, all those, yes."[3] The life of the ancestor can thus be reconsti- of a rock crystal which has been created from five particles of bone or the skeletal remains of the deceased. In this way, the old one returns to the living as a guardian spirit and guarantor of the hunt.

In Australia, the rock crystals introduced into neophytes' bodies in the course of shamanic initiaion, like the Huichol *tewari*, originate in the environs of the sun. "It is into this dangerous sphere, flooded with blinding light and scorching neat, that the *mara'akame* ventures in order to procure the ancestral soul with the aid of the tutelary spirit helper, the Sacred Deer *Kauyumari*." The ancestral soul of the Huichol elder-shaman is captured by a living *ma-*

ra'akame in the fermented maize drink called *nawa*. "And the owner of the deer snare comes close and drinks the *nawa*, the *nawa* in which the crystal was. In which it was caught. It is he who drinks all this *nawa*." In effect, the shaman who drinks the *nawa* in which is found the *tewari* is drinking liquor containing the symbolic bones of a deceased elder-shaman."[4]

There is much evidence of endo-cannibalism in the Americas and Australia where bones and clothing of the deceased are made into drinks and imbibed. In this way, the bond between the living and the dead is revitalized. The crystal, then, as a reincarnated elder, is not only a protector of the hunt, but also a teacher of the living shaman. The *tewari* advises the *mara'akame* on the proper manner in which to conduct ceremonies, the hunt, and life in the rancho. In effect, the shaman is a novice to the *tewari*.

Another point that Furst makes is that the "owner of the deer snare", the one who has drunk the bone liquor of the *tewari* is an elder and headman of a rancho. In former times, headmen were usually *mara'akame* as well. These roles are identified with *Tatewari*, Our Grandfather Fire, who is not only the tutelary deity of shamans but also the very first shaman. This leads us to the notion that the continuity between the living, the wise dead, and ancestral-nature spirits is a primary course for the shaman who is not only intercessor between spirit and human but also a medium for forces from the other world. The shaman is thus the channel for the knowledge of the Ancients, the means for the wisdom of the Elders and Elements to be transmitted to the community.

For the Huichols, the first ancestor was *Tatewari*. In the Paradisical Era before the flood, when people, creatures, divine beings, and gods were not differentiated from each other, he was brought into being by the *Hewixi*, animal-people who later were drowned in the great flood that destroyed the world. *Apii* rubbed two sticks together and from them was brought forth fire which was contained within the wood. Because fire "came forth" first in the world, he is called Our Grandfather.

For it is our Grandfather who brings us life, who brings us warmth. Now in the Huichols' ceremony, such devotion to *Tatewari* is the *central* heart essence of ceremonial behavior. The bringing together of the food for *Tatewari*, the collecting of the wood, is done with a tremendos amount of affection in the ceremony. The lighting of that wood when Grandfather is brought out is something that is attended frequently with much weeping. The feeding of the grandfather in the course of the ceremony is done with *such* affection. One looks into the fire during the course of the cermony, holding the food of Tatewari and there is this *sweet* sense of communication with the old man who is your teacher, and who is constantly transforming, revealing more.

There is much affection for Our Grandfather Fire amoung the Huichols. Anthropologist Barbara Myerhoff notes that on a practical level, *Tatewari*, as fire, clears the fields, cooks the food, and provides warmth and light. He transmutes the raw and makes a civilized life possible. He also symbolically stands for companionship; where he is, so also are Huichols. As the oldest god among the Huichols, the first *mara'akame,* and the shaman of the Ancient Ones, *Tatewari* protects and transmits the traditions of long ago. He is much loved by Huichols for he reveals the unknowable with his light and his wisdom of great age.

The text that follows was given to Dr. Myerhoff by Ramon Medina Silva. The narrative reveals the profound significance of this first elder of Ancient Times:

"Why do we adore the one who is not of this world, whom we call *Tatewari,* the one who is the Fire? We have him because we believe in him in this form. *Tai,* that is fire, only fire, flames. *Tatewari* that is the Fire. That is the *mara'akame* from ancient times, the one who warms us, who burns the brush, who cooks our food, who hunted the deer, the peyote, that one who is with Kauyumari. We believe in him. Without him, where would we get warmth? How would we cook? All would be cold. To keep warm Our Sun Father would have to come close to the earth. And that cannot be so.

"Imagine. One is in the Sierra, there where we Huichols live. One walks, one follows one's paths. Then it becomes dark. One is alone there walking; one sees nothing. What is it there in the dark? One hears something? It is not to be seen. All is cold. Then one makes camp there. One gathers a little wood, food for Tatewari. One strikes a light. One brings out Tatewari. Ah, what a fine thing! What warmth! What light! The darkness disappears. It is safe. Tatewari is there to protect one. Far away, another walks. He sees it. There he is, walking all alone in the darkness, afraid perhaps. Then he sees it from far away, that light, that friendly light. A friendly thing in the dark. He says, 'I am not alone. There is another Huichol. There is someone. Perhaps he has a place for me there, a little warmth.' So he speaks. Tatewari is there in the dark, making light, making one warm, guarding one. Is it possible to live without such a thing, without Tatewari? No, it is not possible.

"Or if it is a matter of working to produce maize, squash, beans, melon. Working is not enough. We need Tatewari. If one has a wife, she wishes to cook for one. How can one satisfy one's hunger with a pot of raw beans? With raw maize? It does not satisfy. But give these things into the hands of Tatewari, let them be warmed by the flower of his flames, then it is well. In Ancient Times he was transformed. When the Ancient Ones brought him out, he came out as *mara'akame*, transformed, so that all could see him as he was. So that he could embrace Our Father when he was born. So that he could lead those Ancient Ones who were not of this world to hunt the deer, to hunt peyote. So that Kauyumari and he became companions, so that our life, our customs could be established there from Ancient Times, so long ago that no one can remember when it was.

"That is why we adore him, why we have him in the center, that one who is Our Grandfather."[5]

A Huichol myth relates that *Tatewari*, one day, found the gods in the *xiriki* or temple complaining bitterly about their ills. They knew not what caused their suffering nor how to rid themselves of disease. Grandfather Fire, desiring to help them, divined that the gods had not made the sacred pilgrimage to *Wirikuta*, the Land of Peyote, for many years. They had forgotten the ways of their ancestors, who had journeyed far to hunt the Deer (peyote) in Paradise, the place of their origin. Forgetting their traditions and obligations to the Divine Ones, so also had they forgotten that to heal they must eat the miraculous flesh of the deer-peyote. And in this way does the *mara'akame*, as Our Grandfather, Tatewari, leads all pilgrims to Paradise to find their Life. This is done every year.

The Huichol shaman's tutelary deity is *Tatewari;* so also is the *mara'akame* identified as Our Grandfather Fire. Like *Tatewari* of the Huichols, Old Woman Momoy of the Southern California Chumash is identified as a mythological ancestor with shaman powers. She is Grandmother Datura, a wealthy widow whose medicine revives the dead and cures the sick. By drinking the water in which she has bathed, one can avoid death. She sets down the rules of conduct and is the guardian of traditions. Her grandson, an orphan whom she raises, grows up to be a powerful shaman and hunter.

Anthropologist Thomas Blackburn notes that age, like knowledge, is highly valued in Chumash society, and , in fact, the two are correlated. With age comes wisdom, and from wisdom comes power. Only the wise can survive to a very old age in a universe that is so dangerous. In the mythology of the Chumash, most characters with power are elderly. Sun, the most powerful of the entities, is depicted as an extremely old man. Eagle, an influential and rarely visible presence, is characterized as both wise and good, the embodiment of normative values. Well-to-do Eagle, as Chief, has great prestige and provides for the community. The one who administers the hallucinatory drug Datura to pubescent boys is Old Man Coyote, a trickster and a shaman who can change his appearance at will. As Blackburn says, authority and power are a direct function of seniority and maturity.[6]

For many Native American peoples, the status of the aged is one of respect and honor. Living to a ripe old age was a priviledge granted by the gods or the Supreme Maker. A life that had been "completed" was one that had passed through *all* stages to the last, the age of wisdom. For many Native American peoples, the elderly had certain rights and privileges. As one Pomo Native American has said, "The old people were important. They were wise."

It is the Elders who have the greatest access to the ancestors and gods. Many years of practice in the ways of the sacred combined with the nearing of death has opened their lives to a manner of spiritual and social freedom. Those who have been favored with long life, from one point of view, have gone through a life-span initiation. The path of life itself when traversed with "an obedience to awareness" is instruction.

The Gros Ventre of Montana believe the elders to be favored, and from The Wise Ones blessings are sought. "If you are good to old people, these in turn will pray to the Supreme Being for your health, long life, and success. Children were instructed explicitly to be good to the aged, to feed them, to clothe and to help them in difficulties, as well as to seek out those so blessed and ask for their prayers."[7]

This change of worlds can be accomplished in life as well as death. The shaman and the Elders understand the fundamental nature of the transformative process. To attain the solar realm, where consciousness is eternally awakened, to climb to the top of the mountain where the infinite is revealed, to Seek Life in order to know death, this is the quest, the journey.

As a child in his Pueblo village, Alfonso Ortiz's vision was directed to the mountaintop, the place where the paths of those living and the dead converge. It is this sacred geography that the shaman attains, and there also are found the Ancestors.

"A wise elder among my people, the Tewa, frequently used the phrase *Pin pe obi,* 'look to the mountaintop,' while he was alive. I first heard it 25 years ago when I was seven years old; as I was practicing for the first time to participate in relay races we run in the Pueblo country to give strength to the sun father as he journeys across the sky. I was at one end of the earth track which ran east to west, like the path of the sun. The old man who was blind, called to me and said, 'Young One, as you run, look to the mountaintop.' And he pointed to *Tsikomo,* the western sacred mountain of the Tewa world, which loomed off in the distance. 'Keep your gaze fixed on that mountain, and you will feel the miles melt beneath your feet. Do this and in time you will feel as if you can leap over bushes, trees, and even the river.' I tried to understand what this last statement meant, but I was too young.

"On another occasion a few days later, I asked him if I really could learn to leap over treetops. He smiled and said, 'Whatever life's challenges you may face, remember always look to the mountaintop, for in so doing you look to greatness. Remember this, and let no problem, however great it may seem, discourage you. This is the one thought I want to leave you with. And in that dim coming time when we shall meet again, it shall be on the mountaintop.' Again I wondered why he was telling me these words and what they meant. I did not have long to wonder why, for the following month, when the cornstalks were sturdy on the land, he died quietly in his sleep having seen eighty seven summers.

"Although he knew I was too young to understand, he also knew there was not much time left to impart this message to me and, perhaps, to others like me. In accordance with our beliefs, the ancestors were waiting for him at the edge of the village that day he died, waiting to take him on a final four-day journey to the four sacred mountains of the Tewa world. A tewa must either be a medicine man in a state of purity or he must be dead before he can safely ascend the sacred mountain. This final journey always ends when the ancestral spirits and the one who has returned enters a lake near the top of any of the sacred mountains, for these lakes are the homes of the gods.

"In the most basic, transcendental sense, then, life for a Tewa consists of trying to fathom the meaning of these words, 'look to the mountaintop', for they contain a guiding vision of life, a vision evolved through untold millenia of living on this land. Only in recent years have I come fully to realize that this was a priceless gift, for it sums up a people's knowledge of what it means to be of a time and of a place, also beyond time and place. Yet I also know that I shall never fully understand all that is meant by these words, for if ever I or anyone living should do so, it would be time to rejoin the ancestors, to make the last journey to the mountaintop."[8]

All of life for an Elder or Holy One is directed toward the attainment of the mountaintop, where a transtemporal geography reveals the infinite. Even the very young are reminded of this sacred possibility. In a Navajo blessing for a child, the medicine man prays that the little one will grow up healthy and strong into the age of wisdom. The blessing concludes with these words: "I am the Essence of Life which is old age."

FOOTNOTES

1. Bogoras, W., The *Chuckchee*, Vol. 7, AMNH, Vol.II, 1904.

2. Laski, V., *Seeking Life*, University of Texas Press, Austin, Texas, 1959.

3. Furst, P.T., *"Huichol Conceptions of the Soul"*, from the journal *Folklore Americas*, Vol. 27, 1967, P. 80.

4. Furst, Ibid, P. 93

5. Myerhoff, B., *Peyote Hunt*, Cornell University Press, 1974, P. 78-80.

6. Blackburn, T., *December's Child*, University of California Press, Berkeley, 1975, P. 74 - 75.

7. Cooper, J.M., *Gros Venture of Montana*, Pt. II, Catholic University of America, Anthropological Series, No. 14, Washington, D.C., 1957, P. 195.

8. Ortiz, A., *Look to the Mountaintops"*, in *Essays of Reflection*, ed. by E.G. Ward, Houghton - Mifflin, Boston, 1959, p. 95 - 97.

WISDOM AND WILDERNESS

Joseph W. Meeker

Wisdom and wilderness are awesome words. They inspire feelings of profound respect, a little fear, and wonder when we recall how little we know about them. It's something like talking about God or joy or love; most people would rather not. These are what engineers like to call "soft" topics, the kind that can't be handily measured or readily applied to the solving of problems. But wisdom and wilderness also happen to be two of the most essential resources for human beings, both necessary to our survival and welfare.

Perhaps practical minds prefer to avoid thinking about wisdom and wilderness because neither is subject to human management. They happen by themselves according to natural processes which are not understood. No educational system knows how to create wisdom, and no science can make a wilderness. We do know how to damage and destroy both of them, however, and we have devoted much of our energy toward doing that in recent centuries. Before we reach the point where both wisdom and wilderness cease to exist, it will be worth our while to think for a moment about what they are, how they relate to one another, and what the world should be like without them.

Wisdom is a state of the human mind characterized by profound understanding and deep insight. It is often, but not necessarily, accompanied by extensive formal knowledge. Unschooled people can acquire wisdom, and it is no more common to find wise people among professors than it is among carpenters, fishermen, or housewives. Wherever it exists, wisdom shows itself as a perception of the relativity and relationships among things. It is an awareness of wholeness which does not lose sight of particularity or concreteness, or of the intricacies of interrelationships. It is where left and right brains come together in a union of logic and poetry and sensation, and where self-awareness is no longer at odds with awareness of the otherness of the world. Wisdom cannot be confined to a specialized field, nor is it an academic discipline; it is the consciousness of wholeness and integrity which transcends both. It is the state of complexity understood and relationships accepted.

Wilderness is to nature as wisdom is to consciousness. It is a complex of natural relationships where plants, animals, and the land are able to fulfill their environments without technological human interference. Wilderness is a systemic complex so intricate that it often appears chaotic to eyes accustomed to simpler contexts such as farms or cities. Whether it is a Ponderosa pine forest, an African savannah, arctic tundra, or a desert of the American southwest, wilderness environments are natural communities of vastly intricate relationships and subtle interdependencies. However great the number of species and forces involved, wilderness environments feel like integrated places where multiplicity makes sense and complex order is evident.

There are good reasons to believe that wisdom grew from wilderness environments. The human brain did most of its million-year evolving long before humans had acquired the ability to domesticate natural systems. It was in response to the conditions of wilderness living that our brains acquired their basic characteristics. The more simplified environments of agricultural life have existed for only a few thousand years, during which time the brain and its functions have not changed the patterns of many millenia of life in the wilderness.

What we have inherited from that history, our multi-leveled brain linked in many ways to our bodily functions and to our natural environments, is a good instrument for comprehending the world in its wilderness complexity. We are capable of perceiving clearly a many-dimensional world, of feeling deeply about it, of relating to one another and to other species in a large variety of ways, of analyzing logically our experiences and thoughts, and of bringing unlikely aspects of our awareness into imaginative new combinations. It appears that we are well designed for wholeness, and that we are equipped for wisdom. Why then, aren't more of us wise?

One reason may be that we spend so much of our lives merely being clever, and cleverness and wisdom don't mix well. It is clever of us to divide our knowledge up into specialized categories which are easy to manage. Cleverness also is evident in our manipulative tools and technology. We cleverly develop our egos at the expense of one another, and at high cost to the natural systems around us. A large portion of each modern life is spent perfecting our identities and leaving monuments upon the world to prove that we lived here for a while. Enmeshed in such a process, we take little time for reflecting upon the context of our lives, and even less trying to understand how the world really works.

Another reason is that we have created for ourselves domesticated and urban environments which lack the species diversity and multiple relationships of natural wilderness. Humanized environments are the only ones most people know. I always feel compassion for the apocryphal New Yorker who lives his entire life in buildings and on concrete, dies and is buried without ever coming in contact with genuine earth. Most of us are not much better off, even when we visit rural countrysides where natural elements are managed for human benefit, or national parks where nature is experienced in a crowded campground or displayed at a visitor center. Such places, however pleasant they may be, are a long way from the wilderness with its many life forms, intricate dependencies, risks and essential indifference to human interests.

An important ingredient in wisdom is the humility that comes from recognition of the trans-human otherness of the world. It is no wonder that saints for centuries have withdrawn from human communities in favor of wilderness settings when they were searching for spiritual insight. Wilderness is an otherness that to many has looked like God, or whatever the equivalent of God might be in their culture. Interestingly, it can also have the same effect upon a scientist who may regard himself as irreligious. Perhaps the common sense of awe in the face of non-human complexity and greatness of scale is the central experience that is felt the same by the religious and the irreligious alike. Whatever the cause, the world has accumulated much testimony that prolonged experience of wilderness is a deepening and expanding experience for humans.

Human cleverness, applied over many centuries in the pursuit of human benefits, has left us with a complicated society, but it has not produced a genuinely complex one. The difference between complication and complexity is crucial to the understanding of both wisdom and wilderness.

Civilization for the past few centuries has had the effect of simplifying the systems of nature and increasing the complications of human societies. "Divide and conquer" has been the slogan as natural processes and elements have been isolated and manipulated one at a time to make them yield maximum benefits for human purposes. This extends ancient agricultural practices requiring that only one crop at a time be grown on land that previously supported complex vegetation in its wild state, or that animal domestication should breed selectively for a few characteristics and try to eliminate wild traits undesirable to human handlers. Specialization depends upon simplification; both have proved to be profitable for humans and costly to the systems of nature.

The profits reaped from simplifying nature have been plowed into increasing the complications of human life. Each new conquest of nature has led to the introduction of new elements into human society. Technology multiplies its products prodigiously, supported by economic theories which encourage the expansion of human wants and needs. The belief in continuous growth is part of the basic ideology of conventional social and economic thought, but little attention is paid to the character or direction of that growth. New elements are thus added almost at random, with little thought for their integration with other elements. As Alice said of Wonderland, things just get complicateder and complicateder.

Complication tends toward chaos, while complexity is highly organized. Complexity is a characteristic of systems in which very many elements are integrated to form a whole. New parts of such systems (e.g., of ecosystems or higher organisms) appear only when there exist suitable niches and adequate resources for their support, so their presence "makes sense" and does not contribute to chaos. Complicated structures tend to be fragile and delicate, as is evident in the booms and busts of modern economies, or in the devastating impact of varying the availability of one ingredient—say, of crude oil. In contrast, complex systems are resilient and relatively stable. They are so constituted that their component subunits, by 'systemic' cooperation, preserve their integral configuration of structure and behavior and tend to restore it after non-destructive distur-bances. In other words, natural systems survive all disas-ters short of obliteration.

Complexity is an essential characteristic of both wis-dom and wilderness. Both are mature states, reached only after passing beyond periods of fragmentation toward higher forms of integration. They occur as the products of accumulated events in a natural progression over long periods of time. Planning and managing are seldom adequate to encourage either wisdom or wilderness, for much of their structure is the product of response to unan-ticipated changes. Error and surprise are more central to them than are logical progressions or achieved objectives. Tolerance for change and for diversity are more characteris-tic of them than are rigid order and commitment to rules. The resiliency of wisdom and wilderness is in large part because they have the capacity to accommodate what is novel into the basic complexity of their structures. As the wisdom of Gandi made room for some necessary forms of violence in his philosophy of non-violence, so do wilder-ness ecosystems tolerate disruptive technological intru-sions for long periods before their essential integrity be-comes compromised.

Achieving wisdom is clearly not for everybody. The world seems to make good use of the few wise people who appear from time to time, so perhaps only a few are needed. Those who do reach that valuable state have clearly passed beyond some of the small-minded perspectives which occupy most of us through most of our lives. Perhaps that passing-beyond is what a midlife crisis is all about. Such a crisis is often accompanied by a vision that effec-tively puts an end to former illusions about personal iden-tity, the meaning of one's work, and of one's relationships with people and other creatures.

A midlife change of consciousness can clear out mental decks, freeing us from the need to be clever in the pursuit of small interests. Clear decks, of course, are not enough, for at that point in our lives we also need some stimulus toward new and healthier perspectives if we hope to grow. Perhaps the later years of life are the most important times to experience natural wilderness, for those years are often accompanied by a readiness for comprehending complexity that is not present at earlier periods of life.

Dante Alighieri, writing his *Comedy* in the fourteenth century, could have been expected to draw most of his imagery from the agricultural Italian landscapes where he had spent his life. But when Dante reached the point at the close of *The Purgatorio* where he needed to describe the Earthly Paradise, he saw it as a wild natural setting, not as a garden or a pastoral scene. The Earthly Paradise is "a divine forest green and dense." Something prompted Dante to avoid the standard Christian image of a cultivated and sunny Garden of Eden where nature is subordinated to people, and to describe instead a complex landscape which "conceives and brings forth from diverse virtues diverse growths."

Diversity is the clearest feature of Dante's Earthly Paradise, felt in everything from the ground "full of every seed" to the intricate pageantry which displays the entire medieval bestiary of symbolic griffons, foxes, eagles and dragons along with the elaborate forms of church and state on earth and the spiritual heights represented by Christ and the heavenly eyes of Beatrice. This Eden is no place of quiet repose, but a busy meeting ground where the processes of wild nature coalesce with those of human intellect and spirit.

Dante's entire *Comedy,* from the barren and lifeless scenes of Hell, through the increasing natural lushness of Prugatory, and the transcendence of Paradise, demonstrates a basic truth: the state of the natural environments in which people live reflect the state of the human spirit. We all find ourselves in just the environments we have deserved, reflecting our values and our beliefs.

We should be instructed by this as we consider our reasons for protecting natural settings and processes. It's not merely a matter of conserving "resources" for human benefit, or of saving pleasing scenery to gratify our senses. Our minds and souls do have their roots in the untamed processess of nature. Preserving wilderness is really human self-preservation.

What better image of old age could we hope for than the prospect of wisdom contemplating wilderness? There are few treasures higher than these two forms of complex maturity. The rest of us need to study and learn from both in an effort to enrich our lives and the world we live in. In the end, wilderness is nature's way of being wise, and wisdom is the mind's way of being natural.

IN THE REDWOOD FOREST
AT ANDERSON CANYON, BIG SUR

John Norton

early day
before time
before hours
before light and dark
without words
before words
before father
mother
before other
before world or earth
before one and two
before me
before you

Aging and Development

JANUARY

William Bridges

January. Janus. The old double-faced god of the Romans. The god of doorways and the guardian of crossings. Looking backward and looking forward. Janus sees the coming and the going. He knows the source and the destination.

This is a time of transition for me, and I long for a little of the god's understanding. I am in that in-between state in my life, having left behind an outgrown but still perfectly serviceable past, and moving toward a future that resists all my efforts to bring it into focus.

Today I am alone at home, watching it rain and enjoying the solitude. The weather turns everything gray, and I can only see a colorless silhouette at the far end of the pasture where tall trees ordinarily loom large and green. If it keeps up, the pasture will flood again, as it did last year. The children are rooting for the rain. They keep asking how much I think it will rain, hoping that a flood will keep them home from school. "Only two inches," Sarah mutters, peering at the rain gauge. "That isn't much! Do you think it could rain five?"

I secretly share their longing for that sort of little catastrophe, although I am also taking care of myself. I have a fire going in the wood stove, and in between bouts of writing I have been making bread. It's heavy, whole-grain bread, the sort that you could live off for a week or two if you got flooded in. I feel a real need for sustenance that doesn't depend on the outside world today—this month—at this time in my life.

My mood today is a strange combination of lostness and coziness. The rain curtains me in, and the creeks are rising fast. It's a time for all creatures to take cover and check their supplies. It's a winter scene of the mind as well as the body.

Janus's backward glance took me through an old photo album last night. I pored over the early snapshots as though they were clues to some mystery. There stands little Billy in the first. You'd know him anywhere: serious and knock-kneed, tummy pushing out the front of the scratchy wool bathing-suit, that was shaped like a girl's one-piece. Here he is, peering into a snail shell; in the next one he is smiling shyly at his father; and in the last, he is chasing cousin Dave up the beach. Each one is the image of the little boy that in so many ways I still am. But none of them held the clue I sought. That lay with the parents, I discovered.

Dad. A dark-haired man in baggy pants and a wide-brimmed hat. And Mother. A sad-eyed woman in a print dress. I looked back at them, dressed in their Depression and Wartime clothes, and I realized that those images are burned deeply into my consciousness. They are more than memories. They are my images of what Adults—real Grown-Ups—are like. As I looked at them, it occurred to me with a shock that somewhere in the back of my mind I was still waiting for adulthood to arrive. (It can't have come yet, you see, because I've never looked like *them*.) When I came to be my father's age, I dressed and cut my hair differently. I never grew up into that smiling man in the rimless glasses and the white pants, the one leaning carelessly back against the '36 Plymouth Coupe. He is the real adult. I'm an imposter.

This is no small discovery for a forty-four year old to make, you know, especially since my first forty years were untroubled by confusing realizations of this sort. But as I said in the beginning, this is a time of transition for me, an in-between time.

I have recently and reluctantly come to the conclusion (to put it bluntly) that I am lost. Not just unsure that this is the right trail, but off any trail whatsoever. I find myself, figuratively, looking for footprints, broken twigs, any sign that someone has been over this ground ahead of me.

I'd like to think that my situation is like those old drawings in children's magazines, captioned WHAT IS WRONG WITH THIS PICTURE? (If only I can study it hard enough, I'll find that the man in the picture has two left hands or that there's a fish in his hair or that he's writing with a carrot instead of a pen.) But even as I hope, I know that my life is written in a far tougher code—and that, besides, there are no answers in the back of my book.

When I turned to follow the backward glance of Janus, I found that there was no simple path from my own past to retrace. The birds ate all the crumbs I dropped, apparently, and somebody must have rolled my labyrinth string back up into a ball. I could yell for help, in hopes that my mother or the third grade teacher or my scoutmaster will come and find me. But then I think sadly: They're not out looking for me—even though I've been gone a long time and it's getting dark.

So, what I need to discover is whether you can be at home in this place or whether you have to find some way back. I need to find whether this situation offers a reality of its own, or whether I have mysteriously left the map entirely with a wrong turn that led into uncharted wilderness.

But one thing at a time. First, I'll snug up the camp a little, because it looks as though I'll be here for a while. Then build a fire to scare away the night creatures. Then get the lay of the land. And then write this note, put it in a bottle, and toss it out to sea in hopes that you will find it.

That reminds me of another note written by a castaway. At thirty-seven, his career as a diplomat and literateur had been cut short by a power shift in his native city, and he found himself unexpectedly cast adrift. He wrote an immense poem, which began,

> In the middle of the journey of our life
>   I came to my senses in a dark forest,
>   for I had lost the straight path.

Dante's discovery was that there was no way back, but that the journey out led down and through. What a stroke of luck he had, though, finding Virgil at the very beginning of his confusion.

I have had less luck with guides, myself. It's true that it's sometimes hard to see the forest for the people lost in it, these days, but real guides, those who have found their own way at life's midpoint, are rare. They tend to strike off at some unfamiliar angle, and they are soon lost to view. All the more reason, then, to pay attention to people like Dante who left a record of their journeying.

In *The Divine Comedy* he says that he was led by Virgil through a gate to the underworld, where the inscription read ABANDON EVERY HOPE, YOU WHO ENTER HERE. That's hard counsel! Abandoning your hopes sounds like giving up, and much of the time it's only my few last hopes that I have left.

It's a subtle difference that seems not to matter much, on my darker days, but the real alternative to *hope* is not *despair* but *trust*. Hope ties everyting to an outcome, and it is that that really matters. Trust, on the other hand, describes the person's relation to the actual process that is going on. Despair is what you get when you lose hope and forget trust.

I came across an old transcript, the other day, of a counseling session I had a couple years ago with a middle-aged man who was despairing in this sense:

I: What's going on with you now?

He: Nothing. That's just it. Nothing's really going on inside me. My words and actions . . . they're not really *me*. I really wonder whether there's anything there behind my facade.

I: You wonder whether there's anyone home in there?

He: Yeah . . . maybe I'm just an empty house . . . nobody home.

I: Who's doing that wondering?

He: I am . . . What do you mean?

I: I mean, somebody is doing that wondering and worrying. I think that you're so busy looking for what you think an authentic person would look like, that you're missing him. You're elbowing yourself aside and saying, "Excuse me, but I'm looking for a *person* in here."

He: But so much of the time I feel phony to myself.

I: Well, right now you feel very real to me—someone who's really concerned about the difference between what he wishes he was and what he feels he is.

He: You mean, there *is* someone home.

I: Sure. The guy who's rushing around shouting, "Anybody home?"

He: I see that, I guess. But I wish that I were somebody a little more impressive than just a person rushing around the house, looking for someone . . . (As I start to reply) No, wait. I know what you're going to say. You're going to say that I'm also the one who wishes that he were more impressive. (We both laugh) That's fairly impressive, I guess.

It is so much easier to remind someone else of these things than it is to remember them. I feel like one of those little dummies in the fairy tales who's told, THERE IS JUST ONE THING YOU MUSTN'T DO. And what does he do? He does it! How can you be so dumb, I wonder? But that's me. These stories concern breaking inner promises, as well, for at a deep level they concern our inability to keep faith with ourselves. They refer to my own difficulty trusting my inner process rather than hanging my hopes on some pre-determined outcome.

So, meanwhile back in the Forest, we've established Rule Number One: abandon your hopes, and trust the process. Which, in this case, is Being Lost. And which is also, Writing From That Lostness. Doing that, Dante wrote his way out of the woods.

His framework was theological and spatial: the downward, darkening rings of Hell, the island-mountain of Purgatory, and the soaring peak of Paradise. My framework is a far more modest one. The road to Hell is closed for repaving and widening, I understand. Besides, my mind turns more readily to time paths than it does to spatial ones. My framework will be the year, one of the most archaic patterns to impress itself on human consciousness. This is January now. We'll see where I am in December.

It says something about my state of things now, if I recall that January was a calendary afterthought. The original Roman calendar, to which we owe many of our month-names and the basic thirty-day month itself, seems to have had only ten months. The year began in March and "ended" ten months later with December. (Septem-, Octo-, Novem-, and Decem-ber were originally, therefore, the right names for what were the seventh, eighth, ninth, and tenth months.) And what about the two missing months—what about this month? Well, that was simply empty. It was non-time.

This emptiness, which is so strange to our modern, Western outlook, was felt to be a natural part of the rhythm of existence. These two months of winter were not empty slots, waiting to be filled as soon as some appropriate content could be found. The period was more like a rest in music. This stretch of non-time was the part of the cycle when energies flooded forth from the void and renewed the dormant earth and all that lived upon it.

The dead time is still there for me, almost as the closed off basement of some old, long-gone building might lie under the pavement of a busy city. My steps echo hollowly as I cross this part of the year, and as I look back through old letters and diaries, I can see that it has always been so. January has always been a low time for me. It is a time of inwardness, marked by mysterious feelings of loss and loneliness. And always I react in my familiar linear way, seeing the downward slope of my path at this point as the beginning of the end: Here it comes, I always think. Here comes all the nothingness and darkness and mess that my care and self-control have forstalled. You'd think that every winter was my first one.

I want this time to go with the current that I have so often resisted, now and throughout this strange year ahead. For as I began by saying, I suspect that my sense of lostness is more than just a phase of the annual cycle. I feel somehow as though I had just awakened from a forty-year dream. (WHERE AM I? HOW DID I GET HERE?) I feel like the old drunk that was washed up and shaved by pranksters and put to bed in a fine room which they told him, when he awoke, was his. Calling him by a strage name, they had him half believing in his assumed identity, until they finally admitted the joke. (O.K., WHO'S THE PRANKSTER? COME ON, A JOKE IS A JOKE. I'VE HAD ENOUGH!)

In a sense, I *have* just awakened from a dream. It's a dream that is at once so corny and so strange that it embarrasses me to admit it. It's the idea that I am really a GREAT MAN, who has spent these past fory-four years doing my share of the common, ordinary work, waiting to be recognized. It is not that I've wanted to be president or to be *famous* in the ordinary sense, where you work your way to the top and then enjoy your well-earned reputation. My dream is far more passive than that. In it, there is, in effect, a messenger riding around somewhere with a glass loafer that will fit only me. Or he's looking for the fellow with the little mole on his left foot: The last Dauphin! he cries, dropping to one knee.

Like any dream, it's the funny bits of irrationality that tip you off to its dreamness. Some of them are insignificant, like my waiting for each day's mail, watching for some stunning announcement of my belated recognition. (FLASH. AP. January 24. Forestville, California. To everyone's surprise, William Bridges, 44, was discovered today to be living in relative obscurity. As one of his neighbors said, "He was a nice fellow, but we never dreamed that he was A GREAT MAN.") I scan all the envelopes, but the Nobel Prize Committee never writes, nor does the College of Cardinals.

A more serious effect of the dream is that it has always offered a strange perspective from which to think of the future. It has led me to overlook the conventional opportunities for activity and relationship, while I awaited the *grand* opportunities. Oh, that isn't quite true, for I have manged to keep a respectable career and a fine family afloat. But beneath all the things I have done in my life, there has been a kind of *waiting*. It is only now that I begin to see how much of my life has been undertaken left-handedly while my real attention was fixed on the possible turn of events that would unfold my destiny.

What a strange hold this dream has had on me, and for such a long time! My mind whirs back into my childhood, and events run backwards through my mind like film being reversed in the projector—the diver arcs back up out of the splash onto the board, the shattered dish leaps up into wholeness off the floor, and the full-blown blossom curves back into its bud. Time runs back to 1945 and summer and a Boy Scout Camp on the shore of a forest lake in Maine.

It is the last day of a two-week session, and we are having an evening ceremony for the awarding of badges. It is beginning to get dark, although I can still see all around the lake. I have begun to lose interest in what is going on, with all the petty details of the final point totals for the Red Team and the Green Team. I am only a Tenderfoot, and there will be no prizes for me tonight. I stare out across the silvery surface of the lake.

There is a canoe out there. I wonder idly who would be canoeing at this hour, and I watch as the paddling figure comes closer. He moves the canoe quickly through the water with long, powerful strokes. I squint against the evening brightness on the water, and I make out the form of a dark-skinned young man with streaks of white paint across his cheekbones and a feathered headband. Dressed only in leather trousers, he leans forward takes long, powerful strokes.

I can't say when I realize what he is going to do, but as he beaches the canoe in front of us, I begin to remember something that has been vaguely rumored all week. The brave has come to pick out the finest scout and to take him away, across the lake for a vigil in the woods—a night alone, far from anyone. I remember hearing that the brave walks silently up and down the lines of scouts until he comes to the chosen one. Then he claps him wordlessly on the shoulder as a sign of selection and paddles him away to a secret place where he will spend the night.

From the moment I realize that the canoe is coming toward us, my heart has beat faster. As he steps ashore, I begin to grow really frightened. I don't know why I am reacting this way. All that I can think of is spending the whole night alone in the woods. And I wonder how it feels to be clapped really hard on the soulder; I decide that the pain itself is part of the ordeal. I begin to sweat. Think of being chosen, of stepping forward alone, out of the mass of others, watched by everyone! Think of the stunning silence, the wordless glances in which everything is said and unspoken. Think of the terrible moment of aloneness as you step into the water and push off in the canoe!

Beneath these darting thoughts, a deeper realization begins to take shape: *It is I that the brave has come for.* This thought drives away all the others, and I stand there numb. My ears ring and I feel dizzy. I don't dare to watch him as he walks along the row of boys. I hear the mosquitoes humming and the faint wash of the tiny waves at the edge of the lake. I shut my eyes for a minute to try to get control of myself, for I am sure that I am shaking visibly.

Then without warning, it is all over. Boys near me are whispering the name of one of the older boys, an Eagle Scout, and I look up quickly to see him climbing into the deepening dusk, a voice begins to announce the instructions for evening cleanup and for the departure tomorrow. The words drone on meaninglessly, and then I am startled by a whoop as the boys break ranks and dash in all directions toward the darkened campsites.

I stumble off toward the woods and my tent, suddenly feeling terribly tired. I am confused by what has happened and by the strange mixture of relief and sadness that I feel. Why did I think that the brave would choose *me*? I was a terrible scout: my best knot was the Granny, and I used illegal frog-kicks after the first twenty-five yards of the Australian Crawl. No one even knew me outside our little group of four tents. Something had to be wrong with me to think something like this. I was only thankful that no one knew what I had been thinking.

I arrive at my tent and find my three tent-mates eating cookies and planning a raid on the next tent after lights-out. I go through the motions of excitement over the plan, and an hour later we surprise and devastate the four boys next door. We get into a little trouble, just enough to give our parents something to talk about the next day. And just enough to quiet my deep thoughts, thoughts that stir so far down in my own darkness that I forget them again for thirty years.

Oh, Janus, doorway god, I think that your forward and your backward sight curve around in some great Einsteinian circle to meet. I look back at that adolescent summer, and it brings me back to this middle-aged winter. I open that door and come face-to-face with myself. Is Dreamworld the territory that lies beyond the doorway, or is it the ground on which I now stand? Have I begun to awaken or to fall asleep? In this empty gap, this night-time of the year, all is strange—yet the strangeness is so familiar that I lose my sense of what is real. I cross this January threshold with the sense that I am entering a new country unawares, like a border crossed in the night. (Why aren't the countries different colors, as they were in my fifth grade Geography book? Perhaps they are. This one looks dark, very dark.)

Oh, Janus, share your foresight and your hindsight with me. How did I get here? And where am I headed?

LIFE HAS NO AGE

Ben Weininger

We are here relating wisdom and aging. I'm not sure what either of them are. An artist friend insisted that I tell him whether I was a wise man. After a silence he insisted again. I said, "I'm a wise man who does foolish things." As human beings we are both wise and foolish at any age.

I am techinally a doctor, a psychiatrist, a psychoanalyst. Actually, these labels, including my name, I do not feel identified with. I am living each day the best I can and responding to the challenges in my immediate area of family, friends, and community as required.

In coming to this meeting, having committed myself to it, an intuitive discovery came into my mind. A young person is full of curiosity and wonder. Many old people in modern times have lost some of their curiosity and wonder. The younger scientists in physics and math make the great discoveries. The older ones make less discoveries. My scientist friend, Dr. David Rioch, suggested that the older scientist accumulated so much knowledge, much of which is no longer true; he feels he knows what can and cannot be done. He has acquired too many pet beliefs. The younger scientist does not realize what cannot be done. He is fresh to explore new areas of the universe.

The older person has many beliefs and much knowledge which once was useful to him as a young person, but may no longer be true and he is resistant to let go of his beliefs and take a fresh look as to how the world and society looks now.

This clinging to the familiar is a trait we all have from infancy onward. In the philosophy of Buddhism, clinging to the familiar is the single cause of man-made suffering. I can say man-made, because accidents out of our immediate control (like being hit by a bolt of lightening) may not be due to our psychology.

We have often wondered why it is that many people feel "old" whether they are twenty or eighty, and yet others retain their zest for living at seventy, eighty or at any age. We have discussed the attitudes and lifestyles which contribute to the feeling of age.

Living is no different at the end of life than it is at the beginning, an analogy I discovered recently as I held a birthday candle in my hand and watched the brightness of the flame at the beginning, and watched it as the candle got smaller and smaller. I noticed that the flame continued to be as bright at the end of the life of the candle as it was in the geginning. Life has no age.

In a nuclear family the child has an underlying fear of being abandoned. Sometimes he is lonely. For the child, For Buber, life has meaning only in terms of everday exis- adult life. I see persons in their 60s and 70s who still feel and fear abandonment, loneliness, and that they will get sick and no one will show any interest in them. There is *some* reality to this, but most of these fears are memories from childhood that have not been worked through.

A baby needs to feel wanted and loved before and after he is born. Once he has this enduring feeling of being wanted in childhood, it remains as an enduring process within, throughout his life. I felt this until I was 27 years old. I had a doctor's degree to practice medicine. My father died; I was left without funds and without any knowledge as to how to relate in the objective world. I had been over-protected. I remained anxious and depressed for three years, although at the time I was working as a resident physician in a private psychiatric hopsital. Then I met Dr. Frieda Fromm-Reichmann, my teacher, who I felt once again accepted me unconditionally. My confidence and faith were restored and never completely lost again for the next 45 years. I am 75 years old. I do not feel disabled, isolated, lonely, and I'm not concerned with death. I've been a heart patient for over 60 years and was preoccupied with death for a long time. In my earlier years I often felt lonely and isolated. In discussing my problems I feel I'm also discussing yours, as I feel all of us have similar problems. What we have in common can be described. Our uniqueness, the very essence of our lives, cannot be described in words.

A sense of identity with the religion one is born into, without its dogma, seems to me to be important in the middle-aged and older person. I was brought up in a totally Orthodox Jewish community; my identity is that of an Orthodox Jew. Religion was part of my every day life. I didn't give it any thought. Then , when I was 21 and a medical student, I had a kind of mystical experience and became interested in other religions and philosophies, beginning with Jesus and later Buddha, Krishnamurti, and Zen philosophy. I've explored these religions for most of my life. It was only recently that I became re-interested in my original Jewish religion, through the teachings of Martin Buber. I grew interested in the mystical form of Judaism through Buber's interpretation of Hasidism. It was more than an interest... it was the feeling of returning to my own religion, a feeling of being part of a heritage. I think that this is important, because most people who deny their religious beginnings are cutting off a part of themselves. In later life, especially, it is improtant to get in touch with one's original religion once again, even though one may not believe in all of the dogma and doctrines. I am convinced that to deny feeling a part of that religion, whatever it is, is a repression of an important part of oneself. We need to realize that we must look to our own background, our own roots, in order to have a life with wholeness and meaning, even though we may have rebelled against it at one time. We must feel a part of our traditions, be they Christian, Jewish, or any other. The mystical experience needs to be experienced, it is difficult to explain. It gives one a sense of feeling whole, a sense of belonging to the world, the universe and to the community. When I first had this experience, it gave me such a feeling of ecstasy and joy that it seemed to erase every other experience... from my new understanding of Hasidism, I see that it is important not to make the mystical experience or the "satori" experience or the "nirvana" experience an end to itself. The awareness of that wholeness needs to be applied and experiemented with, and lived into day-to-day life. Unless we can bring that which we have learned into everyday life, we miss the point of the communal. We are social animals and we need to rediscover the social quality in ourselves.

What is the concern about aging, early retirement, inactivity, isolation, economics, illness, disability, fear and death? One dies of a disease, not of old age. My particular focus of interest is not on the political, social and economic factors involved in the present aging problems, but rather on psychological and spiritual factors and how our psychological attitudes and spiritual orientation relate to the fears of aging, disability, loneliness, isolation and death.

Fear is at the heart of what keeps our character rigid. When we feel threatened we react with fear; it is natural. I have a heart pain. I react with fear. The fear comes and goes. It does not stay.

Fear is derived from the past and projected into the future by our thoughts. There is no fear in the moment.

Fear of being alone, like the other fears, has two aspects to it. First of all, there is an objective real possibility of being left alone, not having any more friends, losing a spouse, having children move to distant places. Secondly, there are inner fears that have not been resolved in early life: fears of abandonment in childhood which have carried over into adulthood and now into old age. This psychological fear is not rooted in reality, but in a basic mustrust of life. We cannot do anything about the reality of being alone or about death, but it is not a fear of physical death or of being alone, but rather a fear of *change*. It is the great fear of the unknown. How we cope with this fear depends on how we have coped with previous changes in our lives.

We are all essentially alone in this universe.

Most of us are afraid of a universal aloneness, of being one small person in a vast and unimaginable universe. We cling to others . . . whether friends, relatives or children. We feel abandoned when we are left alone by divorce, death, or a separation. We have always looked for support from the outside. The feeling of being abandoned is a carryover from childhood. The small child has no other source of support and protection than his parents. The adult has other resources. The adult often needs to be alone. If a person can admit that he is alone in the universe and is not afraid of consciously recognizing this, he becomes part of that universe. This is what I call the "inner community". When you have it, it's difficult to feel lonely. You feel connected with all of life, the life force which some people call God and others perhaps call nature, or many other names. All names refer to creative force in the universe of which we are a part because we were born. Every person needs to recognize that his center of life, his spiritual center, and his feeling of community is in his aloneness. He needs to feel a part of the universe and of nature.

In the Oriental philosophies there is a preoccupation with inner feelings and the inner life to the extent that the objective reality of the outside world is ignored. I believe that if spiritual awareness exists, there is no separation between inner and outer reality. You belong to your family, your friends, your society, and to the universe. The inner reality is your subjective world and it's just as real as the objective outer world.

I believe that most people direct their attention to what the outside world is doing to them, rather than to what the inner world feels like. For instance, some people become depressed when it is raining; it feels like a hostile intrusion from the outside world. Now if one pays attention to one's reactions to the rain, one can get in touch with one's inner life. We need to pay attention to our reactions, because it is there that we create problems for ourselves. Some people overreact to every situation, feeling hurt and depressed in their encounters with others. We need to pay attention, so that if over-reacting is our pattern, we can get in touch with that facet of ourselves and our responses to nature. We must be aware if we are cutting out the sunshine in our lives by how we react to hurts and losses. There's no way of not reacting to those feelings, but we do have some control once we understand our reactions; we have control over whether those hurts go on for days, weeks, or years. We must observe the reaction, and perhaps learn from the hurt and not be swallowed up by it.

We have spoken of turning and looking inward in the second half of life. When the inward journey begins it remains: you never lose what you have begun.

There is also the fear of being empty inside, of not having the inner resources to cope with the world anymore. Often life itself fills up a lot of emptiness; just getting up in the morning, washing, having breakfast, writing a letter; the ordinary things fill up a lot of empty spaces. If a person has been hurt a lot and has built barriers around himself, he will be reluctant to expose himself to others for fear of being hurt again. Then a large part of that person remains hidden, unavailable even to himself. This person is not living fully and probably never has. Such a person would find it more difficult to be left alone than a person who has been able in the past to live fully most of the time. In order to live fully one need not be doing things continually. The great thinkers have been pretty passive and have been dependent upon others to do their "business" for them. Being involved with life is an inner process which connects one to the universe and all that is in it. If a person is living fully now, fear of the future would disappear.

Fear usually involves a concern about the future. Fear of the future implies an unpleasantness from the past projected onto the future. Since you never know the future, you anticipate it from past experience.

If one has a problem with fear, the person needs to know, to look into what is blocking him from living more fully in the present.

Why do some people have faith in life and some do not? Can lost faith be regained? What obstacles are in the way of trust in the life process? Can spirituality and faith be taught by instruction? Can mental and physical illness impair one's faith in life? These are questions that we are studying. The meaning of life is the daily living of it—faith in life, an intuitive trust in the life process.

To feel accepted and inspired to pursue self-knowledge as a life goal, is the direction to rediscovery—lost and found, like a game of hide and seek. The priority of self-knowledge is the key, always in relation with others.

What if a person never felt completely wanted and loved and he meets reverses in life? Can he learn to gain faith in life again? Yes. First, he needs to meet some friend or professional who can restimulate him, to acknowledge in him his essence. The person needs to feel unconditionally accepted. The spiritual energy comes from a deep contact with another person; a feeling of being undonditionally accepted is a spiritual one—a sense of wholeness. This gives us the energy to let go of the thoughts and feelings, so that the mind can be empty of thoughts and reactive emotions, and the heart full.

The fear of economic security is sometimes valid; sometimes a lack of faith. My own inner fear of economic security I see as a lack of faith and a lack of touch with my full life resources. Gandhi said, "Fearlessness is the first requisite of a spiritual life." We can pay attention to our responses to the realities of our lives, and deal with them accordingly.

A great influence in my life was the psychoanalyst, Frieda Fromm-Reichmann. It was Frieda who awakened in me a sense of dedication to both my work and my life. She was the kind of person who usually went a second mile for others—without resentment—and this was her secret. I learned from studying the life of Jesus that going the second mile meant having the genuine willingness to do more than is required, without any resentment. I found this an important key, not only to human relations, but to all of life.

Martin Buber is the last of my teachers. Whenever I read his works, I feel a joy in me that I can hardly contain. For Buber, life has meaning only in terms of everyday existence. Buber also rekindled my feeling for my original religion, because I realized through him that denying our earliest religious feelings often diminishes our lives. I feel comfortable seeing our common humanity through the religious feeling of my childhood, although I do not feel compelled to practice the traditional ceremonies of Judaism.

What makes us feel old and lonely and fearful is the accumulation and fixation of old emotions that have no relevance for our present life, and if we understand ourselves we can see what are the psychological factors that keep us from dropping old hurts from the past. Loneliness and emptiness can be frightening, but if you don't run away from it, loneliness is the *key* to spiritual life. If you don't try to avoid it or fill it out, it is the doorway. If you run away from it then you don't pass through the door. If I am lonely it is momentary; the next hour I may be joyous. Once recognized, emotions need not be expressed, at least not fully expressed. I seldom give expression to them— occasionally yes; usually no. The misconception if that not expressing feelings is harmful. The more accurate view is that if you are angry and don't recognize it, instead you develop a headache. Unrecognized emotions are harmful; others can feel them and see them for us. Our emotional reactions to threats become a problem when we hang onto the emotions, when they become chronic, like hatred, jealousy, vindictiveness, etc. Fleeting emotional reactions are harmless and this is part of being human.

Our emotions are kept alive by our thoughts. We wallow in them. The problems lie in our thoughts and not in the emotions themselves. We dwell on them, think on them over and over again. The thoughts serve a function of keeping the status quo. We are familiar with the emotions and thoughts and are afraid to let go of the thoughts; it is important to have insight into this fact, that it is our thoughts that keep the hurt feeling, self-pity, loneliness alive. Some of us see this, but the thoughts and feelings persist. We don't have sufficient spiritual energy to let go of the thoughts.

When you're depressed, it isn't just being depressed. There is one active thing you do. You *actively withdraw*— that causes the depression. You have a philosophy—your belief system says you are only worthwhile if you are with somebody—if the belief system is looked into and dropped, then you won't have to withdraw. You feel alone because you withdraw. Actually, you're never really alone. There are too many people in the world. An adult often needs to be alone. If a person can admit that he is indeed *alone* in the universe and is not afraid of recognizing this, he becomes part of that universe. This is what I call the "inner community." When you have it, it is difficult to feel lonely. You feel connected with all of life. It is a feeling of a sense of community life; I belong here. I don't have to be with people. I can be alone, yet I don't feel lonely; I *feel connected.*

In the process of aging, if we are to age well, we need to maintain physical health through proper nutrition, exercise, and maintain a weight of less than 10% of what is called normal. Secondly, we need to pay attention to our happiness quotient, our mental health. If we are mentally ill or have manic depression, mood swings, then special treatment is required. For instance, at the present time lithium carbonate is a treatment of choice, along with other treatment.

And for our aging well mentally, it requires:

One: that we need to learn that our emotional reactions (hurt, anger, sorrow, joy, happiness) are temporary and momentary states.

Two: that life constantly tears down our images that we hold dear, and we need to realize that our images of ourselves are barriers to openness, to real relationships without images.

Three: one of the most important things we need to learn is that our reliance on another person for our happiness misses the mark. The Kingdom of God is within you. We need each other, yet the center of our life cannot rely on another person. We need to be self-reliant—being centered in ourselves, yet open to relations to others. Some relations are more important than others, but no other person can be the source of our life. It's too much of a demand to place on another person. If we can live without each other, then we can live together and learn to love each other.

Others can be our guides and inspiration, and only *we* can make our own observations and do our own learning, stand on our own feet, and also be in relationships with others.

In summarizing: To age well requires a maintenance of wellness, mental and physical; to evolve spiritually through understanding our psychological self. The main thing to be aware of is to see how we try to maintain psychological security by trying to hold onto things as they are.

Wisdom is just being aware of and rejecting the things that are dead ends, the values that are not real. For example, a man works hard to get a big house and car, etc. Then as he gets older and wiser he realizes these things do not bring happiness and he rejects them. As we become older and did as a consequence. Life has a way of shoving our

Life is like a river. Don't stop the river. It is always in the process of moving and changing.

An expression of thanks:

To let go of the past,
Yet retain a friendly relation to it.
To let go of one's teachers,
Yet remain in good relations with them.
To let go of one's life and see
That whatever life we had
We touched the Eternal.

                                                    B.W.

PERSONALITY DEVELOPMENT AT 80 OR ANY OLD AGE

Nevitt Sanford

For practical purposes what we need most to know about personality development is what makes a given developmental change take place. I would argue that the ways in which development occurs can be boiled down to two: through challenge and through self-insight. Challenge means simply the presentation of a stimulus situation which requires a new response, or the generation of a new response capacity, which amounts to an expansion of the personality, something which in time has to be integrated with the rest—a process that is assisted, crucially, by self-insight. The challenging stimuli in children and young people are often brought to bear by the process of maturation, which may include some features of cognitive growth. At the same time, we must bear in mind that the normal processes of maturation can be distorted by various kinds of harmful and inappropriate stimuli.

When it comes to the study of adults, knowledge of what mileposts are yet to be passed, and of what, on the average, are the major pressures and possibilities of the stage of life the individual is in can help our understanding of the state of the organism and suggest which stimuli are likely to have which effects with which individuals.

But with individuals we need to know a lot more than

that. What makes it so difficult to get a close grip on the hypothetical stages of development in adults as well as in children and youth is, of course, the dynamic unconscious. Freud and Erikson have bravely set forth schemes to suggest the times when particular kinds of unconscious conflicts are likely to come to the fore; but this is an uncertain business; fresh traumata, resulting in making something unconscious can occur, fortuitously, at any time, and so can the letting up of old repressions.

Adults, all that I have known, like everybody else, are still laboring under a burden of unconscious structures built up, or laid down, in childhood or adolescence.

I knew a graduate student, a 45 year old woman, who had been psychoanalyzed, practiced psychotherapy for some years under excellent supervision, counseled school teachers, raised three happy children, but who still structured her graduate school experience according to a basic pattern established as a child at home: there was always a talented mother who represented high standards but didn't understand her, and a father who understood but wasn't around very much. She was able to modify this structure during the course of her work on her Ph.d. dissertation; but we can well imagine that had she not encountered this special set of circumstances she might still be struggling with this same pattern—this "unfreedom" in interpersonal relations—at 55 or later.

There is reson to believe, however, that in later life, when the responsibilities of family life and career have been reduced, structures of this kind, needed less for defensive purposes, are more easily demolished; or they may crumble on their own. I expect, however, that such demolition will still take some work aimed at self-insight.

This brings us to the old issue concerning the roles of behavior change and of self-insight in bringing about change in personality. And it brings us also to the contemporary issue of how to integrate psychoanalytic and cognitive theories of human development.

Let me say first about insight that it need not be something that comes only in bright flashes; it may be expressed in quite ordinary conscious functioning. Recall my comment on the repeated lowerings of authoritarianism in educational settings; it seems to me that at least by the third time around a person would begin to say to himself "this is where I came in"; remembering things in this way, connecting them with present events, seeing all this in a broader perspective come under the heading of insight as I understand it, and are essential to the integration of personality. But it is quite possible that this by itself would not be enough to change behavior.

I suppose the case of the student just mentioned could easily be used to illustrate the failure of insight—all that analysis, all that immersion in clinical work and still no change in the persisting struture. But is it not instead a story about the difficulty of attaining insight into deeply based processes? I think it is likely that the insight which finally came, and which our student valued highly as a contribution to the integration of her personality, would not have been attained had she not left home and come to a different country, escaped from the network of relationships at the clinic where she worked, entered a situation that provided challenges and resisted the projection onto it of old patterns, and engaged in some new forms of behavior while continuing the work of self-analysis.

What I am saying here is that a developmental change in personality—at any age beyond childhood—occurs not through challenge *or* self-insight, not even through challenge *and* self-insight considered as separate or successive processes, but through the interaction of the two. A preliminary general formulation would be the following:

1. *For a change in personality to occur there must be a change in behavior.*

2. *Change in behavior depends upon the presence of an appropriate and effective challenge, one that is sufficient to upset equilibrium but not so extreme as to induce regression, that is to say, not too severe in an objective sense and not beyond the limits of the individual's adaptive capacities (ego strength).*

3. *In childhood and adolescence there are usually challenges in abundance but for adults the presentation of an effective challenge will ordinarily require a change in the person's general situation–in the social roles, relationships, responsibilities, and reward systems that structure the life and which are, in effect, external barriers to development.*

In our studies of college and university professors it has been deeply impressed upon my colleagues and me that significant changes in behavior are difficult and rare as long as the professor lives and works in the same culture and social structure. For change in an individual professor to occur it appears necessary either that the culture and social system be changed, or that the individual move to a different situation. I believe that the culture and social structure of an academic institution can be changed, albeit by somewhat heroic measures while changes in people who leave their academic positions are readily to be observed. Two more or less retired professors, a woman and a man, joined the staff of the Institute for the Study of Human Problems at Stanford soon after its beginning and immediately began to take a new lease on life. Their gaiety, eagerness to learn, capacity to find excitement in a new venture contrasted sharply with the grim, know-it-all coolness of the striving academics who surrounded us.

People no longer taken up with making a success in the world have a great deal of freedom and, having little to prove, they can afford to take risks; they can be sure that time will bring events such as physical changes and intimations of the approach of death which, to say the least, will be challenging and provide opportunities to find new meanings. And they can be sure, too, that they have some developmental deficits, which can now be made up for. As suggested earlier, old defensive structures, if they have not disappeared are at least pretty brittle.

Some of us were talking about this the other day and one of our students, aged 35, said "Okay, I know plenty of swingers in their sixties, but how do I get from here to there?" She had in mind particularly the demands of family and career. These, we may believe, are often challenges favorable to development and they seem appropriate enough for early and middle adulthood, but one cannot do everything at once and if she or he is aware of needs and potentialities that are not being expressed, current responsibilities may be experienced as barriers to development. But this is to assume that one knows that further development is possible; and this leads to the next point.

4. *Personality development requires the knowledge, or at least the implicit assumption, that one can develop.*

I remember with what amazement, and excitement, Stanford undergraduates learned that their personalities were not forever fixed by their infantile experiences or their current group memberships. How much more difficult, as Jung has said, for adults in our culture to realize that the second half of life can be radically different from the first.

The graduate student mentioned above took my course in personality development while she was working on her dissertation. She said the chance to integrate cognitive theory with her psychoanalytic ideas was very important to the achievement of what she felt was intellectual clarification. It was my impression that she took some lessons from that course very much to heart, finding much in our discussions of adult development that she could apply directly toward the consolidation of the personality integration that was being attained.

I won't argue that didactic work so formal as this is necessary to adult development or that, by itself, it is likely to have much effect on personality. Our culture puts heavy accent on youth and youthfulness and assumes that the second half of life will be lived along lines laid down in the first. We have defined few respectable roles for old people. It seems clear that means must be found to disseminate information about the possibilities of life after 40.

5.   *Knowledge that change is possible, and freedom from external barriers to change, have to be supplemented by positive stimuli to action in order for significant change in behavior to occur.*

The retired professors who joined me at Stanford had not only freedom *from* but freedom *to.* New and interesting things were in fact going on, and their imaginations were captured. They could see opportunities for the use of their special capabilities; and they could see that not only their talents but their wisdom and experience were needed and valued.

6.   *A challenge must be experienced as such, and it must be accepted, if it is to induce durable change in behavior.*

Much of our general knowledge about the succession of developments in personality is based on the fact that we learn from experience and on the fact that it is possible within limits to predict when given experiences are likely to occur. But we have to reckon with the individual's capacity to *have* experiences, There is not much point in offering a European experience to adolescents who are so sunk in ethnocentrism that they can only compare everything they see unfavorably with what they have been offered at home. It is the subjective "definition of the situation" that the individual responds to, and if he is able to transform objectively new situations into equivalents of what he has experienced before change in behavior is not to be expected.

Various kinds of motives and cognitive dispositions enter into the determination of how the individual sees a situation. Looming large among them are unconscious processes. The activity of these processes can prevent the effects which we ordinarily expect to follow from the first four conditions described above. For example, an individual can make an objectively new situation familiar by projecting onto it deeply based fantasies and cognitive structures. Again, apparently potent stimuli may fail to strike any responsive chord because their natural appeal is to needs that have been made unconscious due to their being in conflict with conscience or self-concept. Finally, unconscious needs in various subtle ways interfere directly with knowing, as when a person with a fine intellectual grasp of the possibilities for development resists amy application of this knowledge to himself or herself.

Most commonly, however, the conditions described above touch parts of the person that are *not* dominated by unconscious processes and, accordingly, there is ordinary learning from experience. More than thay, as suggested above, the objective conditions that favor change in behavior also favor self-insight. If there is indeed a change in behavior one can hardly help but notice it; there will be disequilibrium and a sense of tension until conscious effort has brought the new behavior into line with a suitable self-conception. And, arguing from holistic theory, I would say also that if a change in behavior induces change in a part of the personality this will have implications for the whole. If, for example, there is expansion of parts not dominated by unconscious processes there will be a changed relationship between what is conscious and what is unconscious; the latter may now more readily become conscious, or it may dwindle in significance.

Nevertheless, a professional who would assist people with their self-development should be prepared to take unconscious processes into account. If we are ever to arrive at psychological laws that are truly general we must learn how to write unconscious dynamic processes into our theoretical formulations.

7. *Steps can be taken to prevent the projection onto new situations of psychological contents from the past, to overcome resistance to the assimilation of knowledge and to consideration of alternative ways of behaving, and to connect new stimuli with inner needs and potentialities.*

The psychoanalyzed graduate student mentioned above was hardly alone in her tendency to structure her graduate school experience in accord with a childhood pattern of conceptions and behavior. Graduate school is a great stage for the reenactment of family dramas. Given the power of professors over students, and the complex, obscure and emotionally charged relationships among the professors, students are under strong pressure to transfer to their new relationships attitudes and imaging generated in childhood. If one student wants to find both understanding and insistence upon high standards in the same professor (which, come to think of, does not seem to much to ask), another wants to pick fights with all the authorities around, another to play off one professor against another, while still another is thrown into a panic by signs of disagreements among admired professors. Understandably enough, professors by and large resist being drawn into these dramas by remaining aloof and sticking strictly to business - with the result that students complain about impersonality and inability to "get at" these professors. We cannot expect professors to behave like clinical psychologists, but the fact remains that a professor who does permit a student to come close, who understands the nature of the transference being made but does not fall in with it—does not get drawn into a fight, does not reject a student who is asking for it, etc.—can make a deeply significant contribution to that student's development through providing an experience that "corrects" a childish pattern of interpersonal relations and thereby frees the student from it.

It may be hoped that general knowledge of the processes involved in events of this kind will increase, and spread, so that it will increasingly inform not only graduate education but education in general. The same can be said for dealing with resistance to certain kinds of knowledge, and for finding appropriate stimuli that can assure interest and incite to fresh action. The psychologist speaks of the assessment of an individual personality, of underlying needs and defenses particularly, but the kinds of effects he may achieve by this activity can be achieved also through increased human understanding on the part of all who take responsibility for the education or training of others.

Involved here is the development of the educators themselves. It has been suggested above that current relationships, in the family or at work, may act as effective external barriers to development. And we have seen also that when elements of old relationships are successfully transferred to new ones the barriers—now more internal than external - are maintained. I have argued elsewhere that for people in intimate relationships one to another the development of one depends heavily upon the development of the other(s). This holds not only for parent-child and husband-wife relationships, but for those involving psychotherapists and clients, teachers and students, and professors and their peers.

But it is the adult who would develop himself or herself who is at the center of our deliberations here. I assume that all that is done to change that person's situation, or to bring effective positive stimuli to bear will be done with his or her fully conscious participation. And this brings me to my final general point.

8. *Personality development in adults requires self-examination aimed at self-insight.*

I think I have shown (or perhaps I should say admitted!) that great effort to bring about self-insight, as in full psychoanalytic treatment, may not bring about personality integration if there are not at the same time, or later, changes in the person's situation and behavior. Now I must add that no amount of situation—or behavior—changing will lead to personality development in adults if it is unaccompanied by self-reflection. Indeed the strategies and interventions of professionals amount to little more than manipulation, and can be dehumanizing, if the person involved does not understand what is happening and is not encouraged to think about it in relation to the self.

This brings us to a tentative general formulation: *All* the above conditions and processes are necessary to bring about developmental change in the adult personality. Each must be present in at least some degree, although paucity or weakness in one may be compensated for by abundance or strength in the others, and there may be combinations that are optimal—or inappropriate.

When development is seen in this way the idea of stages recedes in importance. Their presumed invariance may readily be disrupted by the bringing to bear of potent external stimuli or by the intrusion of unconscious processes. And to add a final point, touched upon but not sufficiently accented above: *people develop together.* This holds at the interpersonal, organizational, and societal levels. What we see in marital relationships, for example one in which a wife can hardly develop herself because her husband can conceive of her only as a child or as a mother, can also be seen in parent-child, teacher-student, and therapist-client relationships. In an organiaztion such as a school or college, the teachers can hardly develop themselves if the behavior necessary to start the process goes against firmly established authority or against widely accepted group norms. As for the whole society, Heinz Werner pointed out some time ago that the development of an individual is limited by the level of development of his society. For example, in a simple, relatively undifferentiated society the individual who would become complex courts the dangers of deviance. Our society, highly differentiated as it is, must cope today with massive forces toward homogenization due to technology, and to conformity due to political backwardness. These things are bad for various reasons, not the least of which is that they stand as formidable barriers to human development.

This general formulation raises problems for investigation; but I see no point in waiting until the results are in before undertaking programs in adult development. Such programs should neglect none of the conditions discussed above; each of them suggests actions that most adults will find interesting and worthwhile, and that are likely to contribute to personality development.

The possiblities of this approach were brought home to me by some work with adult women—which was undertaken with other purposes in mind and not conceptualized in the present terms. In the middle 1950's my colleagues and I, of the Mary Conover Mellon Foundation at Vassar College prevailed upon 50 alumnae of that Institution to come to the college for three days, in groups of 10, to take part in an assessment that would help us learn something about the lasting effects of a Vassar education. From time to time since then, beginning a few months after the assessment, I have had direct evidence that for more than a few of the women the three days at Vassar was a profoundly significant experience; for some it was a turning point in their lives, the beginning of courses of personal development in new directions.

In trying to explain how and why this happened I would say now that all of the above conditions were present in some degree. The women got away from their usual rounds and responsibilities, at least for a little while; they were among strangers who had few expectations concerning them. In taking part in the various assessment procedures—group tasks, improvisations, games, directed discussion etc.—they did things they had never done before; they tested themselves in various ways, and had a chance to see themselves as others saw them. And then there were interviews, at least four by as many different people, covering various aspects of the alumnae's lives. They were not offered interpretations in these research interviews but, as we were to learn later, they seized their opportunity for self-examination and stock-taking and thereby increased their capacity for continuing self-examination. The most important thing, I believe, was that they had a fully legitimated chance to talk and think about themselves—with people who were objective, interested, and capable of understanding them—without having first to define themselves as ill, incompetent, or in trouble. They were encouraged to talk about their fantasies but not to act them out. The social arrangements for the assessment were, to say the least, unusual; the company consisted of 10 Vassar alumnae and a staff of 11 psychologists and psychiatrist; the staff joined the women at breakfast, lunch, cocktails, dinner and late evening libations, but they did not step out of their professional roles and so encourage projection of transference. Naturally at that time and place we did not offer the women any lectures on the possibilities of development in the second half of life. But the idea was in the air. Since the whole setting was free of any "clinical" actions or expectations, at least as much attention was given to potentialities as to failings. The question "What are you going to do now?" hardly needed to be asked, and I am sure that many of the women got the idea that they could do more with their lives and with themselves. Almost all of those who came back to the college a few weeks later to "hear something of the results" had plans for interesting future activities. They were encouraged.

A worthwhile undertaking would be to compare this kind of experience with the various short-term group-psychotherapeutic or "growth' procedures currently in fashion. This is too large a subject to be gone into here; but I will say that all these short-term procedures ought to be evaluated in terms of the eight points set forth above.

For me the big problem about offering groups of adults the kind of experience the Vassar women had lies in how to bring them together without their first having defined themselves as "problems" or permitted themselves too many great expectations. Perhaps in time the kind of practical theory I have been trying to develop here will find a place in general discussions of education and give rise to various developmental practices in short-term and long-term programs of adult education. For the time being, my inclination is to start as we did with the Vassar alumnae and as Levinson did, that is, ask people to take part in a study of adult development and then with the understanding and consent of those concerned let the undertaking turn into an action research.

And then I would focus on activities that are good for almost everybody—not least on providing somebody to talk to. It has been dawning on me in recent years that not only colege students and professors but ordinary people rarely have a chance to share confidences with anyone, to talk about things that really matter to them, to reveal themselves enough in a relationship so that they can get some sense of how they are perceived by others and so that important ideas and plans can be tested through being put into words. Such is the degree of alienation in our society that we have to think of special arrangements for providing what people who live in genuine communities have—and what we used to have—as a matter of course. When I speak of providing somebody to talk to, however, I have in mind something more than can be had from friends or relatives; I mean the assistance of professionals who can be objective and who can bring to their conversations a framework within which a life can meaningfully be viewed. It is these things that enable the individual to see himself or herself in proper perspective, and to link the past with the present in the kind of stock-taking that prepares for the future.

And so I come back to the interviews—for which there should be plenty of time. Then there might be group interviews, or discussions, in which themes commonly touched on in the individual interviews are made the focus of attention. Later, perhaps, one might prepare some situations that present special challenges, or bring to the fore long buried defenses or strivings. I would not omit, the stage having been set, didactic materials on the problems and possibilities of aging, nor the discussion of practical arrangements for providing new challenges and interests in actual life.

In concluding, I want to say one thing specially about older people—as my title suggests I was going to do. It will have been recognized, I hope, that when I say "adults" I mean adults of any age. But there are special things about adults in the late decades of life and I will mention one: old people, in our culture, are inhibited and unwanted philosophers. Or perhaps I should say they are inhibited because philosophy is unwanted. Development in the second half of life has been neglected, I believe, because psychologists who study development are a relatively young lot. Bursting with energy and bent on making careers for themselves, they carry out rigorous investigations, using as subjects the people closest to hand—children, students, and people like themselves. Older psychologists interested in development become philosophical about it, but they have no audience nor any ready vehicle for transmitting their ideas. Yet development is very largely a philosophical problem. Consider: I have been assuming all along that development is a good thing, that it is indeed an over-arching value in the sense that the interrelated virtues that stand high in the great ethical systems depend on high levels of development. I have assumed, with John Dewey, that what we do now for others or for ourselves ought to be evaluated not only according to humanitarian principles and the short-term satisfaction of all concerned but in the light of the implications of present actions for future development, and for our culture as a whole. Am I on the right track? Let us ask the old ones. Let us, in imitation of those great cultures, past and present, that relied and rely on the wisdom of the elders, set our older scholars and scientists to work on neglected questions of value. We may hope they have reached high levels of development (my assumption again); if not we may expect them to rise to the challenge and so develop themselves now.

VIRTUE IN OLD AGE

Elizabeth Léonie Simpson

Der mentsh iz voz er iz, ober nit voz er iz.
(A man is what he is, not what he used to be.)
Yiddish Proverb

The question as to whether human beings are born sinners or become corrupted into evil while maturing in a decadent world has never been settled. Nor is it likely to be. It has not, however, been evaded and, with the cyclic frequency of contagious disease, recurs in religious contexts as well as more secular ones. From time to time scientific interest in the subject has arisen and in the process of being structured and legitimized has dealt with explorations into prosocial or altruistic behavior as well as the destructive or the bad as conceptualized or performed throughout the life-span.[1] To a large extent, these inquiries have focussed on the acquisition of conscience in childhood and early maturity through the utilization of new intellectual processes and the internalization of new roles and values. Although developmental theories do, in form, encompass the later and last years, in fact much has been intuited and very little systematically studied about morality and/or moral development and behavior among the elderly.

And even these private intuitions have been beclouded by ambiguity and contradiction. Do people indeed change with their later maturity? In his *Principles of Psychology*, William James asserted that, by the age of 50, an individual's character had set like plaster and would never soften again. But others have believed that there is no such thing as an immutable person, that throughout the life-span we are each involved in a never-ending process of interaction between our internal life and the external social-cultural world and that change, in one form or another, is incessant. From clinicians trained in psychoanalytic perspectives (such as Buhler, Jung, Maslow, Sanford, Rogers and Erikson) have come theories of life-long growth and development which are opposed by a biological model of youth and maturity, followed by active decline.

Does personality continue to develop even during the years characterized by decrements in biological functioning? Lawrence Kohlberg[2] pointed out the convergence of stage theorists such as Erikson, Piaget and himself in suggesting the possibility of positive development among the aging. The cognitive-developmental model of structural change described by Piaget was subsequently modified by Kohlberg to include qualitative differences in modes of thinking which have an invariant sequence and are integrated hierarchically. More than simple age-stage is posited in Erikson's[3] characterization of the last stage of life, shaped and modified by all that has gone before, as the period of *integrity* versus *despair*. Developmentally, old age is a new phase of human experience, one which draws upon the socioenvironmental effects of the past as well as those of biological change. At the seventh stage of *generativity*, Erikson's ideal human becomes the ethical parallel of Kohlberg's Stage 6 thinker who utilizes a structure of universal ethical principles to make moral decisions.[4]

No current formulation presents the whole truth about morality in old age. There is very little theory that is grounded in evidence and where there is, as Bernice Neugarten[5] has pointed out, it is "totally inconsistent". Researchers agree only on the fact that *introversion* (which some see as a symptom of personal disengagement from life) increases as time goes by. Erikson's final stage does not challenge the concept of *disengagement* directly, but is centered on the achievement of responsible renunciation and closure. The discrepancy between empirically testable concepts of moral development and abstract, utopian ones developed philosophically suggest the need for a reality-oriented model with the extremes of *real* and *idealized* behavior interacting. The maintenance of consistent, cross-issue moral maturity is more of an ideal than a practical possibility.

Implicit in both Piaget's and Kohlberg's theories is the belief that the most advanced state of moral development attained will be maintained throughout the remainder of the life-span. But research has indicated that, as the result of neurological decrements, regression to earlier modes of cognition takes place. Lower levels of moral development might be expected in old age and, in fact, a curvelinear relationship between mean moral stage levels and age has been found.[6] Some people become *less* ethical as they age, not more so.

Is old age, then, a time of stasis, of fulfilment and growth, or one of regression and characterological disorder? Our cultural imagery presents opposing answers both as acceptable truths. One is that of aging as continued development into knowing, accompanied by self-acceptance, peace and wisdom. The second is the reverse of this positive one. It is an image of deterioration and decay marked by failure of memory, body and social roles, a defiance of the inevitable which does not prevent self-rejection or its manifestations in irritation, superficiality or plain silliness. In modern society with its predilection for youth and vitality, mythologies laid out in dogmatic propositions of contrast.

When a popular writer, Joan Didion, asks in an essay called "Self-Respect", "What can be more arrogant than to claim the primacy of personal conscience?" and goes on to

insist that "we have no way of knowing—beyond fundamental loyalty to the social code—what is 'right' and what
is 'wrong', what is 'Good' and what 'Evil'," the reader is
forced into a cultural *cul-de-sac*. If morality is what society
defines it to be and aging itself is a sociosomatic illness, the
person has no choice in the matter. Trapped by their self-
acceptance of learned expectations, the elderly are far from
immune to infectious stereotyping. Neither are the members of the helping profesions whose tasks involve interaction with them. The beliefs and opinions of both groups are
shaped by negative attributions made to the oldsters' social
role by others. By middle age most people have internalized
a social clock whose consensually-validated readings use
age-appropriateness as a reasonable criterion for evaluat-
ing all behavior: what is expected is not the same at different times of life.

The "dire dimensions of a final thing" that the poet
Theodore Roethke described have been learned as a ritual
in youth and continue as damaging orthodoxy through the
end of life. From early childhood social limits are placed on
the freedom to imagine oneself as a positive actor in old age.
Findings from a recent study[7] by the Annenberg School of
Communication at the University of Pennsylvania show
how effectively prime-time television programming portrays old men as evil and older women as bad, eccentric or
foolish. Few complaints came from elderly watchers, however, since accepting a stereotype for others is easier than
for oneself, even if it intrudes in everyday interaction.

Reality is more complex than the presentation of
dichotomous poles of growth and regression suggests. Age
is not a leveler of individual differences and personality
organization may be the pivotal factor in the ability to adapt
at this time and how that adaptation is done. Is ethical
commitment liable to cynical revision as the years pass? Or
immorality or illegal behavior subject to "burn-out" over

the passage of time? The fact that prisoners over the age of 50 account for only 5% of persons under correctional supervision suggests that the latter is so[8]. May, then, one become a "better" person by default? By the *reduction* of energy and other personal resources? *The Need to Know.* Can nothing, Ferard Manley Hopkins mourned,

> ... be done
> To keep at keep at bay
> Age and age's evils?

Knowledge allied with understanding is a monumental defense barely begun to be built. What do we need to know about aging and moral development that can be learned by systematic inquiry within the person and between persons as they grow older? A comprehensive and appropriate framework, based on evidence and not intuition, is still lacking: so are the data which are needed to complete such an outline and give it vital relevance to the possibility of socially supported personal change towards the end of life. What is presented here as a resource (and hence intended as provocation) is some intellectual and emotional unfinished business in human underdeveloped territories. The list is by no means complete; nor are the catagories mutually exclusive. They are labelled as *Cultural Differences, Mental and Physical Health, Autonomous Morality, Environmental Factors, Self-Concept, Family Relationship and Sexuality, and Social and Personal Aaptation.*

1. *Cultural Differences.* In different cultures how is immorality defined in relationship to the doer's age (as well as sex and social status). How do judgments and responses differ: Meg Greenfield, for example,[9] told how women arrested for adultery in Pakistan are not flogged in public if they are over 45 years of age: they have their faces painted black instead.

2. *Mental and Physical Health* In 1975 a Louis Harris survey [9a] found that surviving oldsters tend to be less lonely than younger people—only 12% of those over 65 felt that loneliness was a very serious problem. While this may be only the result of biological disengagement, it may also be because the lonely have *already* died. Some investigators have suggested that negative feelings (such as loneliness) increase altruistic action because individuals learn that this is self-gratifying behavior. More needs to be known about loneliness as death-precipitating as well as a factor affecting other kinds of behavior.

To what extent do mental and physical deterioration (including pain) affect moral behavior? Under what conditions do they produce personal growth which motivates more ethical interpersonal contact? Does imagination—as an evolving phenomenological construction of reality—become more negative and anxiety-producing?

3. *Autonomous Morality.* We still know too little about the variables which affect personality change in later life. Are there fundamental, lasting prosocial or anti-social dispositions, residing in individuals as general states or traits, which are inherited or established in early life and maintained to its close? Is it possible that, for some persons, maturation to the stage of autonomous decision-making may not be accomplished *until* old age? That conformity to conventions may be abandoned then?

Do those who have achieved moral autonomy earlier in life maintain it until death? If the wicked die young and the good live long lives (as the ancient Hebrews believed), there should be no temptation to misbehavior at life's close. That is not always the case although past reputation may alleviate the consequences of these new ways of acting. Is there less concern among the old about *justice* as a widely applied abstraction than as a matter of benefit to oneself and one's loved ones? Is each ethical problem responded to as unique rather than as multiple and recurring? Or is the response the result of "knee-jerk" habit by this time?

4. *Environmental Factors.* Both how individuals reason about ethical issues and how they behave are dependent upon personal development but, as researchers have become increasingly aware, they also are strongly influenced by interpersonal interaction and environmental realities. Behavior is situationally based; it is not made in social abstraction or isolation. The current social environment for the elderly is undergoing a stage of massive modification as the proportion of those living within that catagory increases. The range of alternatives is broad and widening: *institutional life, second-generational family residence, retirement community* or *individual separation.* The benefits and liabilities of each are stoutly asserted with very little supporting data which relate to changes in behavior.

Do public or private institutions inevitably foster developmental deprivation?[10] Do homogenous units, socially isolated from other age-groups, need to be automatically disfunctional for continued development? Is helping behavior in such an environment inhibited by the presence of other potential helpers? Does the choice for such segregated living remove responsibility from the aged through the constriction of a controlled fantasy world? Max Lerner has expressed his opinion that the "most pernicious form of segragation today" is age-group segregation. The effects of this legitimized escapism are not fully understood. It is easy to see it as a reaction to views of the old which were widely held not long ago are still influential:

> The functionlessness of the aged is a permanent fact of our society . . . A high value on youth, or overestimation of youth, is inherent in a democratic society such as ours.[11]

Requirements and pressures vary over the life-span and, along with personal utility, morality may be expected to change. Irving Rosow[12] has suggested that "aging should be attended by fewer normative requirements and more options than earlier adult life stages". Because few crucial positions are occupied and the scope of responsibility for others has dwindled so drastically by this time, relatively few *prescribed* norms may be expected to apply in old age. But if some pattern areas of action are less insisted upon, some also may become inaccessible. Access and denial are supported by social pressures and Rosow has pointed out that:

> There are no significant expectations and roles for him. In this sense, an old person's life is basically 'roleless', unstructured by the society, and conspiciously lacking in nor, especially for nonfamilial relationships. [13]

Are the differences in moral development in adult life far more impressive *within* age groups than *between* them—as Campbell[14] found for political development? The lack of cohort correspondence suggests that age may be irrevelant to individual differences.

5. *Self-Concept.* It may be, as Milton claimed in *Paradise Lost*, that

> The mind is its own place, and in itself
> Can make a Heav'n of Hell, a Hell of Heav'n,

but the social environment has a powerful impact upon the mind's assessments. The tendency to idealize the high prestige of the aged may be accompanied today (as it has been in the past) by a less idyllic reality. [15] When those who do not work are not valued, when productivity lags and status is diminished, self-esteem suffers - sometimes with life-denying results. [16] If the old feel no fulfillment or satisfaction - only a sense of separation from the personas and doings with which they were earlier involved - they may easily come to think if themselves as what one writer has called "a throw-away bottle". Even those who have believed in their own integrity and worth may be threatened.

Research data on the quality of self-concept in the old continues to be contradictory. Not all reports are of negativity, and all that seems clear is that social ideology necessarily influences the ego ideal: if the old are valued, they will tend to value themselves. Other factors may also be involved. Grant,[17] for example, found personal denial associated with a self-concept that was more positive than that in other age groups. Doing for others may well be doing for oneself. Some investigators believe that high self-esteem represents a useful defensive reaction and adjustment to old age. In a broad analysis Kaplan and Pokorny[18] have concluded that, while socially and self-sanctioned disengagement supports the maintenance of self-esteem, the experience of social expectations beyond the ability to live up to them is associated with attitudes.

How is self-esteem related to behavior toward others? In a study of the relationship between self-esteem in the aged and their altruism, Trimakas and Nicolay[18a] commented on the "heightened sensitivity of high self-concept scorers to social influence" and found them more altruistic than those with less self-esteem.

Does the relationship between helping, considerate and donating behavior and personal competence, social responsibility, and initiation of social interaction—all variables reflecting self-confidence and ego strength—continue to be manifest in old age? What is the elderly person's *subjective* definition of "goodness" and "badness" in conduct? Of "moral health"? How would each one describe him- or herself using these definitions? What do they believe is the appropriate reaction to observed or proven wrong-doing to others or to themselves: *retaliation, constructive leeway (e.g., confession and reparation for the damage done); unqualified forgiveness;* or *careful attention to the preven-*

tion of future, similar acts? How do they defend these beliefs—that is, what do they believe would be the social outcomes of acting upon each of them? Are there social class differences in the choice for self-direction (as opposed to conformity to external authority) consistent in old age?

Do the aged believe in personal responsibility for their own behavior? In responsibility for their social environment? What are the self-concepts of members of the Gray Panthers or other socially active organizations such as the Foster Grandparents? And from that question comes the larger one: who among the elderly choose to involve themselves in the remolding of a world in which they will have limited participation? In an era of diminishing personal capacity this choice represents a powerful ethical stance.

6. *Family Relationship and Sexuality.* The interaction patterns of biological family members change over time, with women expecting more in the way of filial responsibility in old age than males do.[19] Re-integrated into the household, the once-independent parent may become a live-in baby-sitter whose opinions, if solicited by adults, may never be taken as the final word. Physical fraility may be unwittingly interpreted as senility when younger family members assume that aging and intellectual deterioration are one and the same. In this close setting identity and self-respect—and along with them, moral authority—may be routinely and subvertly diminished. Both aged parents and adult children may see dependence as immoral.

For some, the geographical isolation of the nuclear family offspring may leave the aged emotionally stranded and liable to seek companionship in re-marriage and the formation of new ties.[20] The continuance of an active sexual life may be relatively simple under those circumstances but it often is not—for the same, crippling reason: guilt and shame originating in the stereotype of desire's early flight.[21] It is supposed to be gone and, if it is not, its possessor may be intensely uncomfortable with him- or herself.

When privacy is lacking, residents in nursing homes protect themselves from the sense of loss by denying that sex is needed or enjoyable in later life. In one study by Kass,[22] the majority of respondents didn't feel sexually desireable anymore and their major mode of sexual expression was trying to remain physically attractive. However, another recent study[23] found those interviewed in nursing homes to believe that sexual activity was age-appropriate but they were not involved because of the lack of opportunity. Sexual thoughts and feelings were commonly reported. Ronald Blythe,[24] has recorded the insistence of the middle-aged on believing that the sexual passion of the old is spent. Those who don't want to be considered "nasty", "silly", or "dirty old men or women" resort to self-protective concealment.

Other issues of sexual morality may appear when old-sters and youngsters become emotional cohorts allied against the middle generation. On occasion, this alliance may develop into physical intimacy. The exploration of incest is another on-going area of research into the family relationship of the aged. The grandmother/grandson episode seems to be very rare. Nor do the incestuous grand-fathers reported fit the "dirty old man" stereotype. Perceived as passive and devalued, they are neither senile, psychotic, mentally defective nor drunk. Four out of five are from middle-class backgrounds. No violence is involved; all are gentle and none attempt intercourse with a prepupertal grand-daughter. Perhaps *because* of their gentleness, the grandchild cooperates with them.[25]

A psychotherapist specializing in incest problems reports that grandfather/granddaughter cases comprise 10% of her professional load.[26] She sees the incidence as much a social problem as a private one: the acts motivated at least in part by the pit of helplessness and loneliness into which the elderly have fallen and the increased need for affectionate attention and physical contact. If Forward's hypotheses is correct, there should be no evidence of incestuous involvement on the part of these same actors earlier in life; to date this remains an essentially unexplored question.

7. *Social and Personal Adaptation* Brim and Wheeler[27] state that socialization after the formative years is concerned with *overt* behavior and not with basic values because of the high social cost of re-directing these values when they are unacceptable. Partly to avoid the expensive effort of modification, an age-related re-definition of acceptable behavior may occur. This may be accompanied by an adjustment in the public presentation of self.

After retirement, individuals who are outside the competitive arena have less need to conceal the negative aspects of their personalities. Revealing the sins of the past doesn't present a social obstacle if no competition will occur in the present or a future which is no longer indefinite. Such revelation may be purposeful. The redefinition of the self as a clever nonconformist can be a reaction to the loss of status, to not being taken seriously. Past deceits, daring, sly triumphs can be recalled publicly or even invented in exaggereated embroideries which may be regarded as trivial or unimportant and responded to indulgently by the listener. Real violations of conventions may become commonplace and, in fact, expected by others; they may not be taken seriously and confessions of deviancy may become a sort of boasting, like adding on a few years of life—instead of subtracting them - when age is given. [28] This aberant behavior is not threatening to others because the elderly deviant is not perceived as influential or controlling. Case studies of this kind of adaptation could provide insight into the routinization of deceit and social reinforcement for it.

Socially, the oldster has exceeded the statute of moral limitations applying to narcissistic self-indulgence. Lying may increase for any of the reasons it is done earlier in life: to mislead or deceive in order to take advantage of another, to keep one's own social appearance intact or to glorify it. Adrienne Rich's[29] rationale for women's lying at any age applies to both sexes in their later years: "She's afraid that her own truths are not good enough . . . The liar fears the void". (Lying may also be done for another reason: because some threads of the fabric of memory are worn away, they may be supplied by subtle spinning concocted of both reality and fantasy. Told repeatedly, the growing cloth metamorphorses into truth; its complex origin, forgotten. And then the ethical question is settled: the liar who does not lie on purpose maybe senile or a fool but he or she is not a sinner.)

Self-indulgence in the form of the abandonment of delay of gratification can easily be seen not as a pathological regression to childhood but as a realistic adaptation to the limited time that is left for life. How it is expressed may sometimes raise moral questions about geriatric delinquency but the need itself does not. With limited futurity, present barter for later benefits ends.

Conclusion: Mussen and Eisenberg-berg[30] state candidly, "In brief, the nature of the early development of prosocial behavior is unknown". Nor is its manifestation in late life understood. Cognatitive restructuring of moral thinking seems to be more related to years of formal education than simply to the passage of time.[31] Differences in adult groups are not just different points on the same track: they are more likely to represent diverse ones - tracks which have been altered by historical and societal changes.

A comprehensive theory of life-span morality would have to include both biological and cultural factors and within the latter such variables as family and educational socialization, the mass media and situational determinants. At this time it is easier to state what we are lacking than to be satisfied with present knowledge: we need motivational data, data on the last years and phases of life which include the influence of socialization agents (in the home, among peers, cultural heroes and more), to know more about the interaction among antecedent variables of morality, *i.e.*, predispositions toward certain kinds of behavior. We need accurate explorations into the being of functional altruists and humanitarians—multidimensional assessments which include clinical and naturalistic study using depth interviews, projective and cognitive tests and autobiographical writings which report relationships as well as self-evaluation.

In the next twenty years the questions raised here will become increasingly relevant and their answers— hypothetical or factual—the basis for personal and social policy decision-making. With the population of the elderly steadily expanding there are already indications of attitudinal and value shifts: the biased culture is changing. The *Personal Growth* model of aging advocated and implemented by Gay Luce in the SAGE program has marked a shift in ideology which includes the redefinition of the aged. Pleasure-giving and -getting have been legitimized as aging's "single most important" learning.[32]

Does this necessarily imply the growth of a narrow, hedonistic ethic? Rather, what is projected is an inclusive, vitalizing one supporting not *stasis* but the never-ending renewal of self-assertion and social engagement through the rejection of restrictive behavioral norms: an ethic of the older person striving to live and die meaningfully. If what is done is only for *now*, its value should be intensified, not diminished.

If wisdom is not intelligence but knowledge, if virtue is what is done and not what is professed, then both the aged wise and the elderly good can be identified, encouraged, and emulated. Decline and decay are no longer exclusively appropriate foci for contemporary research. Like real wisdom, actual ethical behavior seems to be concurrent throughout the lifespan with struggle, both emotional and intellectual. Can the accumulated past be made much more actively a component in adaptation to the present and planning for the future? For the sake of both the immediate person and those who follow, introspection should be shared and the role of *cultural* historian become accompanied by that of the *life* historian—the recorder and transmitter of past choices, values and decisions. Perhaps we may learn, as Goethe wrote in *Faust*, that

> This is the highest wisdom that I own,
> The best that mankind ever knew:
> Freedom and life are earned by those alone
> Who conquer them each day anew.
> Surrounded by such danger, each one thrives,
> Childhood, manhood, and age lead active lives.

FOOTNOTES

1. Questions of gerontological morality are of two distinct types: one, *social* problems involving ethical action toward the elderly and the other, problems of *personal* experience—ethical choice applied to individual behavior.

This discussion will be confined to the second of these. For one approach to the first category, see Marquis (1978).

Marquis, Donald. Ethics and the Elderly: Some Problems In S. Spicker; K. Wordward; and D. Van Tassel (Eds.), *Aging and the Elderly: Humanistic Perspectives in Gerontology* Atlantic Highlands, NJ: Humanities Press, 1978, 341-355.

2. Kohlberg, Lawrence. Stages and Aging in Moral Development—Some Speculations. *The Gerontologist*, 13 (4), Winter, 1973, 498-502.

3. Erikson, Erik. *Dimensions of a New Identity.* New York: Norton, 1974.

4. Kohlberg (1973) has since added a "metaphorical notion" of a seventh stage philosophically rooted in a cosmic or infinite (as opposed to a universal humanistic) perspective. It is developed in a movement out of despair into non-egoistic, contemplative experience.

5. Neugarten, Bernice. *The Psychology of Aging: An Overview, JSAS Catalog of Selected Documents in Psychology,* 1976, 6(4), 97. MS. 1340.

6. Bielby and Papalia quality their findings by suggesting that

   It is possible that variability in the moral judgements of the elderly could in part be a result of the 'identity crisis' associated with aging, the onset of senility and social isolation. (p. 305)

   Bielby, Denise and Papalia, Deanne Ellen. Moral Development and Perceptual Role-Taking Egocentrism: Their Development and Interelationship Across the Life Span. *International Journal of Aging and Human Development,* 6 (4), 1975, 293-309.

7. Anonymous. Annenberg Study Finds TV Presenting Highly Distorted Images of the Elderly. *Behavior Today,* 10 (39). October 8, 1979, 2-4.

8. United States National Criminal Justice Information and Statistics Service. *Sourcebook of Criminal Justice Statistics.* USCPO, Washington, D.C., 1977.

9. Newsweek magazine, Fall of 1979

9a. Harris, Louis and Associates. *The Myth and Reality of Aging in America.* Washington, D.C.: National Council on the Aging, 1975

10. Erber, Joan. The Institutionalized Geriatric Patient Considered in a Framework of Developmental Deprivation. *Human Development,* 22, (3), 1979, 165-179.

11. Slater, Philip, Cultural Attitudes Toward the Aged. *Geriatrics*, 18 (1963), 308-314.

2.& 13. Rosow, Irving. *Socialization to Old Age*. Berkeley: University of California Press, 19

14. Campbell, Angus. Politics Through the Life Cycle. *The Gerontologist*, 11, 1971, 112-117.

15. Lipman, Aaron. Prestige of the Aged in Portugal: Realistic Appraisal and Ritualistic Deference. *Journal of Aging and Human Development*, 1 (2) May, 1970, 127-136.

16. Miller, Marv. Suicide After Sixty. *Aging*, November-December, 1978, 284-29, 28-31.

17. Grant, C.H. Age Differences in Self-Concept from Early Childhood through Old Age. *Proceedings*, 79th Annual Convention, American Psychological Association, 1969.

18. Kaplan, Howard B. and Pokorny, Alex Aging and Self-Attitude: A Conditional Relationship. *Journal of Aging and Human Development*, 1 (3), July 1970, 241-250.

18a. Trimakas, K.A. and Nicolay, R.C. Self-Concept and Altruism in Old Age. *Journal of Gerontology, 29 (4), 1974, 434-439.*

19. Seelbach, Wayne. Gender Differences in Expectations for Filial Responsibility. The Gerontologist 17 (5), 1977, 421-424.

20. Vinick, Barbara. Remarriage in Old Age. *The Family Coordinator*, 27 (4), October 1978, 359363.

21. Barash, Dorothy. Sexuality in the Aging: Is There Life After Sixty? *Meninger Perspective*, Spring 1977, 4-11.

22. Kass, Merrie Jean. Sexual Expression of the Elderly in Nursing Homes. *The Geontologist*, 18 (4), August 1978, 372-378.

23. Wasow, Mona and Loeb, Martin. Sexuality in Nursing Homes. *Journal of American Geriatrics,* Spring 1977, 4-11.

24. Blythe, Ronald. *The View in Winter.* New York: Harcourt Brace Jovanovich, 1979.

25. It should be made clear here that the definition of incest currently being used includes much more than actual physical intercourse. Grandfather aggressors may seek manipulation, not penetration. They may use subtle forms of seduction: many were reported who used a fairy tale format, weaving tales of fantasy around the penis and anthropomorphizing it into a being with human characteristics.

Meiselman, Karin. *Incest.* San Francisco: Jossey-Bass, 1978.

26. Forward, Susan and Buck, Craig. *Betrayal of Innocence.* New York: Penguin, 1978.

27. Brim, Orville and Wheeler, Stanton. *Socialization After Childhood.* New York: Wiley, 1966

28. A recent study reported by Richard Mazess and Sylvia Forman (1979) disclosed that the residents of the Ecuadorian village of Vilcabamba were prevaricating about their age bu *increasing* it when they reached the age of 70 in order to attain the greater prestige. They were claiming lifespans equal to those of *Old Testament* patriarchs, but the stated age of 100 was estimated to be equal to an actual age of 84 years.

Mazess, Richard and Forman, Sylvia. Longevity and Age by Exaggeration in Vilcabamba, Ecuador. *Journal of Gerontology,* January 1979, 34 (1), 94-98.

29. Rich, Adrienne. *On Lies, Secrets, and Silence: Selected Prose 1966-1978.* New York: Norton, 1979.

30. Mussen, Paul and Eisenberg-Berg, Nancy. *Roots of Caring, Sharing, and Helping.* San Francisco: Freeman, 1977.

31. Rest, James; Davison, Mark; and Robbins, Steven. Age Trends in Judging Moral Issues. *Child Development, 1978, 49,* 263-279.

32. Dangott, Lillian and Kalish, Richard, *A Time to Enjoy: The Pleasures of Aging.* Englewood Cliffs, NJ: Prentice-Hall, 1979.

ITHAKA

by Constantine P. Cavafy

Setting out on the voyage to Ithaka
You must pray that the way be long,
Full of adventurers and experiences.
The Laistrygonians, and the Kyklopes,
Angry Poseidon, - don't be afraid of them;
You will never find such things on your way,
If only your thoughts be high, and a select
Emotion touch your spirit and your body.
The Laistrygonians, the Kyklopes,
Poseidon raging - you will never meet them,
Unless you carry them with you in your soul,
If your soul does not raise them up before you.

You must pray that the way be long;Many be the summer mornings
When with what pleasure, with what delight
You enter harbours never seen before;
At Phoenician trading stations you must stop,
And must acquire good merchandise,
Mother of pearl and coral, amber and ebony,
And sensous perfumes of every kind;
As much as you can get of sensous perfumes;
You must go to many cities of Egypt,
To learn and still to learn from those who know.

You must always have Ithaka in your mind,
Arrival there is your predestination.
But do not hurry the journey at all.
Better that it should last many years;
Be quite old when you anchor at the island,
Rich with all you have gained on the way,
Not expecting Ithaka to give you riches.
Ithaka has given you your lovely journey.
Without Ithaka you would not have set out.

Poor though you find it, Ithaka has not cheated you.
Wise as you have become, with all your experience,
You will understand the meaning of Ithaka.

-translation
John Mavrogordato (translation)
G. Valassopoulo (penultimate 5 lines)
Joan Stetson (last line)

Creativity and Community

AGING AND THE CARING COMMUNITY

Maurice Friedman

Grow old along with me,
The best is yet to be,
The last of life
For which the first was made.
                    Robert Browning, "Rabbi Ben Ezra"

Our most typical association with aging, in our culture, is not wisdom, serenity, fullness of life, or bringing in the harvest, but a long, terrible period of increasingly failing powers. This image is not based on observation so much as it is on dread, on anticipation of one's own helplessness at the onset of aging. This anticipation was already clearly present in T.S. Eliot's earliest published poem, "The Love Song of J. Alfred Prufrock", written when he was only seventeen!:

I grow old... I grow old...
I shall wear the bottoms of my trousers rolled.

Shall I part my hair behind? Do I dare to eat a peach?
I shall wear white flannel trousers, and walk upon the
          beach.
I have heard the mermaids singing, each to each.

I do not think that they will sing to me.

Eliot was, of course, trying to portray a general alienation and futility, but the form in which he did so was the failing powers of age. This was still more explicit in the first of his 1920 poems, "Gerontion", the fictitious central character of which is an old man awaiting death who realizes that he has not really lived:

>   I an old man,
> A dull head among windy spaces.
>   . . . .
>   I have no ghosts,
> An old man in a draughty house
> Under a windy knob.

We have liked to imagine that death confers some dignity and meaning in the manner of the Greek tragedies. But when this old man's life protracts itself into death, no closure or meaning is to be found:

>   Think at last
> We have not reached conclusion, when I
> Stiffen in a rented house.

All that he can say is that perhaps the failing powers of age are less poignant than the presumed rising powers of youth since age, at any rate, offers no illusion of meeting, no hope of contact with real life:

> I have lost my passion: why should I need to keep it
> Since what is kept must be adulterated?
> I have lost my sight, smell, hearing, taste and touch:
> How should I use them for your closer contact?

At the age of forty T.S. Eliot incurred Edmond Wilson's ire by writing "Ash Wednesday" as if from the standpoint of an old man resigning the powers of youth:

> Because I do not hope to turn again
> Because I do not hope
> Because I do not hope to turn
> Desiring this man's gift and that man's scope

> I no longer strive to strive towards such things
> (Why should the aged eagle stretch its wings?)
> Why should I mourn
> The vanished power of the usual reign?

"Ash Wednesday" is, to be sure, a religious poem of purgation, in contrast to the Waste-Land world depicted in the earlier poems; yet the theme of age as associated with failing powers is as central here as there.

We might hope for something more positive from *The Four Quartets*, Eliot's greatest and most mature summation of human existence. If we are not entirely disappointed in this hope, nonetheless the burden of Eliot's plaint about aging remains the same. We are told in "East Coker" that old age was not "what one had expected." Yet as portrayed here it seems to be almost exactly what Eliot had expected all along:

> What was to be the value of the long looked forward to,
> Long hoped for calm, the autumnal serenity
> And the wisdom of age? Had they deceived us
> Or deceived themselves, the quiet-voiced elders,
> Bequeathing us merely a receipt for deceit?
> The serenity only a deliberate hebetude,
> The wisdom only the knowledge of dead secrets
> Useless in the darkness into which they peered
> Or from which they turned their eyes
> . . . . .
> Do not let me hear
> Of the wisdom of old men, but rather of their folly,
> Of belonging to another, or to others, or to God.

These negative thoughts on aging have, of course, a positive context, the limited value of the knowledge derived from experience, the recognition that "The only wisdom we can hope to acquire / Is the wisdom of humility," the purgation and descent into the dark night of the senses and of the soul. Yet the final stanza of "East Coker" is only a little more promising than the earlier lament, as far as age is concern:

As we grow older
The world becomes stranger, the pattern more
        complicated
Of dead and living . . . . .
Old men ought to be explorers
Here and there does not matter
We must be still and still moving
Into another intensity
For a further union, a deeper communion
Through the dark cold and the empty desolation,
The wave cry, the wind cry, the vast waters
Of the petrel and the porpoise. In my end is my
        beginning.

In "Little Gidding," the crown and recapitualation of the other three poems in *The Four Quartets*, the mystic serenity is punctuated by an Ecclesiastes-type irony at the fruits of old age:

Let me disclose the gifts reserved for age
    To set a crown upon your lifetime's effort.
    First, the cold friction of expiring sense
Without enchantment, offering no promise
    But bitter tastelessness of shadow fruit
    As body and soul begin to fall asunder.
Second, the conscious impotence of rage
    At human folly, and the laceration
    Of laughter at what ceases to amuse.
And last, the rending pain of re-enactment
    Of all that you have done, and been; the shame
    Of motives late revealed, and the awareness
Of things ill done and done to others' harm
    Which once you took for exercise of virtue.
    Then fools' approval stings, and honour stains.

Once again, the context of this bitter refrain is the need for purgation—to be "restored by that refining fire / Where you must move in measure, like a dancer."—and the deeper meaning that may open itself to our exploration so that we can "arrive where we started / And know the place for the first time." Age, then, is not a bad preparation for mystic realization precisely because it is the inevitable preparation for death, as Eliot makes clear in "The Dry Salvages":

> There is the final addition, the failing
> Pride or resentment at failing powers,
> The unattached devotion which might pass for
>   devotionless,
> In a drifting boat with a slow leakage,
> The silent listening to the undeniable
> Clamour of the bell of the last annunciation.

The "last annunciation" whose clamor we cannot deny is, of course, death. Many dread age because it represents the threshold of death with an inevitability that does not attach to any other time of life, unless one is struck by a fatal disease. This is an unassailable insight if for no other reason because our life is future oriented and our movement toward the future, in one sense or another, must take place in hope. Yet for the aging there is no future, no hope except for death—if we stick to the moving finger of time on the surface of the sphere and do not descend, as Eliot bids us, into "the still point of the turning world." We cannot deny "the undeniable clamour of the bell of the last annunciation" even if we hold immortality or reincarnation as a trump card in reserve. Yet a deeper examination of our attitude toward death lays bare that it is not the event itself but our relation to it that terrifies us. Our dread of *both*— aging and death—is rooted in our lack of organic community, our alienation from nature and time, as I have pointed out at length in the chapter on "Death and the Dialogue with the Absurd" in my book *The Hidden Human Image:*

> Man's attitude toward death has always been
> bound up in the closest way with his posture vis-a-vis
> nature, time, and community. Although he is aware of
> the seasons, modern man hardly lives in the time of
> nature. His time is abstract, calendrical, and
> conventional, and his relations to nuture are more and
> more detached—whether nature be the object to be
> exploited, the scene to rhapsodize over, the terrain for

a holiday from the city, or the great Earth Goddess that was only recently celebrated every year to ward off the threat of pollution and ecological imbalance. As a result, it is hardly possible for modern man to see his own death as a part of the natural rhythms and cycles of nature, to be accepted with the wisdom of nature itself . . .

Like K. in Kafka's novel *The Castle*, modern man's attempt to find a foothold in present reality cannot succeed because he is always using the present as a means to some future end. This functional relation to time is caused in turn—and reinforced—by that sense of isolation, rootlessness, and exile which makes modern man feel, in moments of awareness, that he knows no real life. He is cut off from the nourishing stream of community; the prospect of his own death takes on an overwhelming importance that robs life itself of meaning . . .

Certainly, even in the best of communities, death is an individual affair. Even in traditional religions, the journey of the soul to some Hades or Sheol must be facilitated by the community through *rites de passage*. Death *is* that uttermost solitude of which every other abandonment is only a foretaste, as Martin Buber suggests, and time *is* a torrent carrying us irreversibly and inexorably toward "the starkest of all human perspectives"—one's own death. But our obsession with our own deaths, our focus upon them, is in no small part caused by our exile and isolation in the present. This same obsession leads us to use our cults of youth, of having "experiences," of realizing our potentials, as ways of not looking at the facts of old age and death. Our culture gives us no support in hearing Hopkins' "leaden echo" of old age in which we give up all the "girl-graces" of youth in favor of that vision in which every future is cut off except death. Yet this fear of time, old age, and death is woven into every moment of our existence, so that we have no real present and no real mutual presence for one another.[1]

Old age and death are not the same; yet in our imagination and in our anticipations they are inexorably woven together. Our fear of aging is not to be explained by our fear of death. Both have deeper roots in our relation to existence itself, particularly in our culture in which an organic flowing with the Tao often seems an impossibility. Our experiences of abandonment in old age are a foretaste of the uttermost solitude of death; yet our fear of death is itself based upon our fear of abandonment. And *that* fear is based upon the fact that we are already, in some important sense, abandoned. This is nowhere better illustrated than in the existentialist philosophy of Martin Heidegger. Human existence, or *Dasein*—being-there—is, to Heidegger, *zum Tode Sein*—being toward-death; for it is only the resolute anticipation of one's unutterably unique and non-relational death which individualizes *Dasein* down to its own potentiality and frees it from the power of *das Man*—the "They" of ambiguity, curiosity, and idle talk. Granting that our anticipation of our death is a present reality that enters into every moment of our existence, I would nonetheless hold that Heidegger seems at times to forget that what is given to us, hence what is *existentially* of importance, is not the actual *future* moment of death but the *present* moment of anticipation. Putting it another way, Heidegger takes the half-truth of separation that the knowledge of our unique and individual death imparts to each of us and makes it into the specious whole truth of our existence being "ultimately non-relational." But this non-relational quality of our existence is, above all, a fact of our isolation, our estragement, our inability to live in organic community with nature and our fellowmen. T.S. Eliot's *Gerontion* has lost the possibility of contact through the failure of those senses that once enabled him to reach out to others, but the fundamental reality, as he recognizes, is that there was already little possibility of real contact even when his senses were fully empowered.

What can we do in the face of this situation? Medical science has not yet reached the stage where it can indefinitely postpone old age and death. Nor is there sense in railing at the modern person for *not* being organically con-

nected with nature and the human community. We must
ask, rather, what resources, if any, are left to us to accept
age as the best that is yet to be, "The last of life for which the
first is made."'' This is only possible if we can attain a new
and active relation to aging which no longer makes it
merely a time of renunciation, resignation, and purgation,
a la "Ash Wednesday," but sees it, instead, as the ground
for a new beginning. In "Sailing to Byzantium" W.B. Yeats
had pointed to that new beginning in a spirit close to Eliot's
Four Quartets, namely as a renunciation of the physical in
favor of the spiritual, the flux of life in favor of the timeless
and the eternal:

I

That is no country for old men. The young
In one another's arms, birds in the trees
—Those dying generations—at their song,
The salmon-falls, the mackerel-crowded seas,
Fish, flesh, or fowl, commend all summer long
Whatever is begotten born, and dies.
Caught in that sensual music all neglect
Monuments of unaging intellect.

II

An aged man is but a paltry thing,
A tattered coat upon a stick, unless
Soul clap its hands and sing, and louder sing
For every tatter in its mortal dress, . . .

III

O sages standing in God's holy fire
. . . .
. . . be the singing masters of my soul.
Consume my heart away; sick with desire
And fastened to a dying animal
It knows not what it is; and gather me
Into the artifice of eternity.

How sublimely Yeats himself contradicts this sublime and
rarefied spirituality in his final poems on "Crazy Jane"
where the full reality of mortal and sensual life is given its
due!

We should like to know something more and better than this trading of physical life for spiritual life; for that was always open to us, and to reserve it for old age is obviously a *pis aller*, making the best of a bad bargain.

Martin Buber tells of how his concern with folk-schools brought him together with the noble old thinker Hans Natorp in the years immediately following the First World War and in so doing gives us a hint of a fuller understanding of what it might mean to begin anew:

> At that time I was happily surprised at how the man with the steel-grey locks asked us at the beginning of his talk to forget all that we believed we knew about his philosophy from his books. In the last years, which had been war years, reality had been brought so close to him that he saw everything with new eyes and had to think in a new way. To be old is a glorious thing when one has not unlearned what it means *to begin*; this old man had even perhaps first learned it thoroughly in old age. He was not at all young, but he was old in a young way, knowing how to begin[2]

What Natorp achieved, from Buber's report, was clearly not the renunciation of one of his functions or powers for another but a new integration, a new totality, a new and greater wholeness than any he had previously achieved.

Carl G. Jung has the virtue of having been the first to call our attention to the mid-life crisis in which the contraction of body and psyche can lead not to despair or simple renunciation but a new integration and individuation in which the deeper goals of the person are fulfilled. There are many existential crises in life and they come at different times. The mid-life crisis might be described as an existential crisis that is an organic and inevitable part of adult development. This does not mean that it comes at the same time or in the same way for all persons who are growing older, much less that they respond to it in any similar fashion. However, what Adrian Van Kaam says of existential crises can be applied to the crisis of aging, namely, that it involves the three phases of psychological death, decision, and rebirth, that it entails the frustration of facing one's growing limitations, and that, if the person does not fall into illusion or despair, it means seeking new, more realistic goals, renouncing old dreams in order to be free to pursue new ones, giving up old unrealistic self-images but also creating new, more mature ones.

To the Protestant theologian Paul Tillich, the non-being that threatens us in the existentialist crisis must be transcended through an essentialist faith which enables us to receive the grace that accepts us despite our being unacceptable. I believe, in contrast, that an existential crisis must be met by an existential response. Mystic experience and religious faith may give us an *essential* trust, but they cannot give us *existential* trust. Yet only existential trust provides us, in the language of my book *Touchstones of Reality*, with the "courage to address and the courage to respond." An essential part of this courage to address and respond is the willingness to begin anew. Without existential trust one cannot make a new beginning, and without it being old cannot be "a glorious thing."

> The trust in existence that enables us to live from moment to moment and to go out to meet what the new moment brings is the trust that makes it possible that in new meeting we again become whole, alive, present. If I trust in a person, a relationship, this means that despite what may and will happen, I shall enter into relationship again and bring all the past moments of meeting into present meeting. The particular person who is my partner may die, become sick, disturbed; he may betray me, rupture the relationship, or simply turn away and fail to respond. Sooner or later something of this does happen for most of us. When it does, it is trust which enables us to remain open and respond to the new address of the situation. If we lose our trust in existence, conversely, we are no longer able to enter anew into real dialogue.[3]

The existential mistrust that gets in the way of our beginning anew is probably with us from our earliest childhood experiences of separation and betrayal, and it is enormously heightened by the smog of existential mistrust that polutes our culture. But surely it is in the time of aging that it is most difficult to begin anew for all but the exceptional few. It is in this time that we experience the attrition of our energy and powers, and loss of our hope, *and* the loss of confirmation by significant others and by the broader community. At the age of sixty the enormously prolific and creative Austrian novelist Stefan Zweig joined with his wife in what the Germans call *Freitod*, a joint suicide in which they carried out their resolution to leave life at the height of their powers rather than experience the waning into age. *Zweig* did not think that old age was the time of serenity and wisdom. It was, for him, the time of the loss of power and control. If we flowed with the Tao, we would not, to be sure, be so concerned with power and control. But it is precisely *this* existential trust which is largely lacking in our culture. Old age is like sleep in that it means, in the language of Peter Koestenbaum, a *deconstitution* of the ego, a letting go, a trust in others, a willingness to be dependent. We begin with such a dependence and trust in childhood, but to end with it in our "second childhood" is more than some of us can contemplate; for we doubt with good reason that there is much to depend upon.

My mother actually drew up a legal document in which she stated her insistence that she not be put into a nursing home, or what used to be called an "old folks' home" when she grew old. My sister with whom she lived nonetheless found it necessary to put my mother into such a home for the last four years of her life. The last time I saw my mother alive was in the home of my sister in Wichita where we all celebrated the sixtieth birthday of my older sister who had come from Florida for the occasion. We were all enormously gratified at how lucid my mother was. She spoke of how strange it was to her to have a daughter of sixty, made a beautiful little speech, and presented each of her three children a check. To me this was especially wonderful since when I had seen my mother two years before she had just had a stroke and did not even recognize me. My younger sister and I took my mother back to the nursing home fifteen miles outside of Wichita. When she got out of the car, my mother stumbled. By the time we got her into the nursing home, she no longer recognized me! Two years after my mother's death, this same sister broke down weeping at lunch and told me how racked with guilt she was for having put my mother in the nursing home even though it seemed, at the time, the only possible thing to do given my mother's penchant for lighting fires under pots with nothing in them while no one was at home. She also told me how afraid she was that some similar fate may await her when she gets to be my mother's age *and* that my mother's youngest brother chose to commit suicide at the age of eighty after his three older sisters had all died.

Perhaps because I was not as closely tied to my mother as my sister and did not have responsibility for the decision to put her in a nursing home, I have not dwelled much on thoughts of guilt or fears of my own approaching old age. On the other hand, at a much younger age than my mother did, I have acquired a habit of losing things and frantically searching for them! I have always rather looked forward to my retirement as a time when I can write without outside impedimenta. But I have occasionally asked myself whether there will not be by that time *inside* impedimenta by way of loss of energy, anxiety, illness, or whatever other ravages age may bring. I suspect that the answer to this question depends upon my own ability to begin anew. Can I learn to live in closer tune with my body? Can I take up the writing of a novel where I left off thirty years ago and launch a whole new direction in my writing? Or is such creativity reserved for the intensity of youth which makes up for its lack of perspective and direction with an overabundance of energy?

Carl Jung was certainly not concerned with an essentialist answer to the existential question of aging but wished, rather, to find a wholly existential one. His own life, as we encounter it in *Memories, Dreams, Reflections* and in the films taken of him is his old age, is impressive testimony to his having achieved an existential wholeness and strength greater than his more youthful ones. What is more, Jung has supplied us with a rich literature of myth and symbol that serves as a useful counterpoise to the undue emphasis of our culture upon youth.

Yet there is one aspect that Jung and the other explorers of midlife crisis and the crisis of aging have ignored or under-played. That is the aspect of community. Most of Jung's myths and symbols are drawn from earlier, more organic communities than any that exist now. What is more, they represent the communal *confirmation* of the individual who is going through these rites of passage. Such a confirmation is largely absent in today's culture, and no amount of Jungian therapy and books richly studded with the myths and symbols of the past can make up for this lack. The existential crisis of the person who is aging in our culture is neither an entirely individual one nor is it simply an affair of one's inner life and one's dreams.

Overcoming the crisis of aging depends, we have suggested, upon beginning anew, and the ability to begin anew is a function of our spiritual life in detachment from the whole of our existence. It is, we have suggested, that which makes possible the courage to address and to respond anew even when "the conditions are no longer propitious' and those we have formerly addressed and responded to in our lives have long since fallen away. The dread of old age, as we have seen, is inextricably bound up with our sense of alienation and isolation from real community. After the death of one Hasidic rebbe, a friend of his said that if he had had someone to talk to, he would still be alive. It is also bound up with the fact that our culture does not confirm the powers of age but only those of youth. We do not look to the Confucian scholar, the rabbinic sage, the aged *staretz*, or the wise old man as our sources for communal wisdom but to the successful young executives, the bright young governors, and the movie stars who are still in their prime. When John Fitzgerald Kennedy became President of the United States, everyone was impressed by the fact that youth was at last at the helm. The shock that reverberated through the nation and the world on the day of his assassination was in no small measure connected with the destruction of precisely that symbol.

On that very day I went to a celebration in New York in which Loren Eisely and my own professor and member of my dissertation committee Charles Hartshorne were awarded the LeConte de Nouy Prize for their work on bringing together religion and science. I had not seen Hartshorne in some years, but I had been in correspondence with him in my role as editor of *The Philosophy of Martin Buber* volume of *The Library of Living Philosophers*. Hartshorne wrote the essay for our volume on Buber's metaphysics, and he began it with the statement, "Buber is no metaphysician, Buber is one of the greatest metaphysicians." Then, as one would expect of the greatest disciple of Alfred North Whitehead, he remade Buber's philosophy in the image of a "Process and Reality" approach to metaphysics. When Buber replied, he wrote, "Dear Hartshorne, I have read your essay attentively several times. I am afraid that we can only agree on the first of your two propositions, 'that I am no metaphysician'." In the short paragraph that followed Buber rejected the metaphysician's insistence that one must choose between a God that is absolute and a God that is relation. Instead Buber spoke of God as the "Absolute Person" who is in relation with man and the world. When I spoke with Hartshorne during the reception following the presentations, this invariably mild-manner man expressed an anger that I had never witnessed in him. This did not bother me, but I was disturbed by his statement, "Buber must be getting senile!" Instead of considering that there might be a real difference of approach here worthy of understanding, however much he might disagree with it, Hartshorne, himself already in his seventies, wished to lay what angered him at the doorstep of Buber's advancing years.

Buber was not senile then or even later. Despite the failure of his eyesight and repeated illness, he continued his work on revising the fourth edition of his translation of the Hebrew Bible into German until he entered his final coma. In the summer of 1946, when he was sixty-eight years old, Buber attested in his Preface to his new collection of Hasidic tales that by far the greater part of it was written since his arrival in Palestine in 1938. Buber attributed his ability to begin anew to his relationship to his new homeland:

> Along with much else, I owe the urge to this new and more comprehensive composition to the air of this land. Our sages say that it makes one wise; to me it has granted a different gift: the strength to make a new beginning. I had regarded my work on the hasidic legends as completed. This book is the outcome of a beginning.[4]

Buber did not, to be sure, receive the confirmation in Palestine, later Israel, that he had in Central Europe. Still, for all his controversial stances and the relative isolation that they brought, he knew there too the meaning of connection with community.

No person is so totally self-sufficient that he or she can live without this confirmation, much less make a new beginning. Kierkegaard's "knight of faith" who knows the solitary relationship of the Single One to his divine Thou cannot be a model for us; for it ignores the existential trust that depends on one's participation in community and one's relations to one's fellow men. Dostoevsky's Prince Myshkin is a more realistic portrait. There is something genuinely terrifying about the ending of Dostoevsky's novel *The Idiot* that cannot be resolved or alleviated. Prince Myshkin's suffering points us to the dreadful question of whether a person can find the highest meaning in a lonely suffering in which he is not only abandoned but unconfirmed; whether he can continue *as a person* to follow a path in "fear and trembling" without the grace received from others that enables him to be human. Socrates, to be sure, was able to persevere in his life-stance at the age of seventy, even when the majority of Athenians disconfirmed him. But he had a large minority that backed him and a group of faithful disciples who remained with him until the end. Jung too, for all his great individual strength, was deeply confirmed by a large community of disciples. Without the confirmation by others in community one can make no meaningful new beginning in response to the crisis of old age.

Yet we have already stressed the lack of the organic community of the past in our present culture. My sister's guilt about my mother was triggered, in part, by her hearing of the way in which old people are treated in other cultures, such as the Netherlands. This treatment depends upon the existence of extended families, which are more and more becoming rare in this culture, or upon a community consciousness of shared responsibility which we are almost totally lacking. The old, like the insane, the retarded, and the criminal, are to be put out of sight so as not to disturb that pleasant idyll in which the rest of us choose to live! Relatively few grown children today consider it their responsibility to take their aging parents into their homes and care for them as they were once cared for by these same parents when they were children. Reciprocity between the generations is largely understood as passing on to our children the advantages that our parents passed on to us.

We cannot go backward to the organic community of the Middle Ages or even to the extended family systems of a few generations ago. But we can, we *must* go forward to a new type of community if the "gray panthers" are to have their day in court. This new community is what I have called the "community of otherness" or the "caring community."

The "community of otherness" is a term I coined out of a shared experience of five years with The Working Party for the Future of the Quaker Movement. In it I became conscious of the enormous difference between a community of affinity, or likemindedness, that is bound together by a common formula, creed, or social condition, and a community of otherness in which the real boundaries of the community are drawn no more narrowly than the reality of the community itself, *including* all those who do not seem to "fit in" or be contributing, respectable citizens. What makes community is people finding themselves in a common situation—a situation which they approach in different ways, yet one which calls each of them out. The very existence in community is already a common concern, a caring for one another. But part of the problem of aging, we have already see, is the reluctance of the rest of the community to acknowledge that the old *are* in a common situation with them or that they are properly objects of a communal concern which is not pity or charity but a vital aspect of community itself. "When people age they lose the sense of the I-boundary in which they are invested, "the Gestalt therapists Erving and Miriam Polster have said. This is because aging necessarily means a *contraction* of the boundary of the self. But is this undermining of the self, which seems to be a contributing factor to so much senility and gerontic insanity, really necessary? A program for senior citizens in San Diego concerned with educational growth opportunities has as its acronym "EGO." It is clearly an attempt to create a community of otherness that will help to confirm the self of the senior citizen which the ordinary structures and clutures of our society disconfirm. Abraham Joshua Herschel suggested at a White House Conference on Aging that there should be senior universities where the old could learn for the sake of learning. Another program for the aged in San Diego is appropriately called "Lifeline."

The lived reality of the community of otherness can come into being wherever persons meet in a spirit of common concern, ready to encounter one another beyond their terminologies and beyond their differences in age, social position, and culture. No group is able to confirm all otherness. That is beyond human capacity. But the test of a fellowship is the otherness that it can confirm. It should not begin by going out to gather other people in but by understanding from within the actual people present. If we tell the aging, by work or glance or action, that their day is past, that they have nothing essential to contribute to the culture, that they are no longer really a part of the ongoing community, then we have read them out of existence as effectively as possible and hastened the spiritual death that so often precedes the physical one. It is our lack of trust, our existential mistrust, that makes us feel that we have to have the security of groups, based on the general affinity of similar existential and social conditions rather than on the concreteness of open meeting with the real otherness that is present in every group.

I am not calling for new legislation any more than for a better moral attitude toward the aged. The "community of otherness" implies a relationship that takes place *between* persons and cannot be counted on as a social technique at our disposal. We live in a time in which we find ourselves painfully trying to rebuild real communities within the larger social bodies. One of the dangers, of course, is the temptation to betray the "community of otherness" by designating one's own commune or cell "the blessed community" and consigning everything else to total meaninglessness, if not to the profane. Everything is the "real world," including the "godforsaken" part of it. The distinguished family psychiatrist Ivan Boszormenyi-Nagy has shown that our connection with our parents and grandparents is not only an organic and inescapable one but is also the only real avenue open to us for reestablishing trust in our society and healing the breaches in relationship and in self that we carry with us and impart to our own children and grandchildren.

The perspective of the "community of otherness" must extend beyond the family to the community and even to that hoped-for community-of-communities that our agglomerate society might one day become. Reality is not given in me alone or in some group or community, with which I identify myself in opposition to the "they" who stand outside. The respect for the otherness of the other does not mean that I love everyone or even that I have the resources to meet everyone in genuine dialogue. But it does mean that just everything that confronts me demands my attention and response—whether of love or hate, agreement or opposition, confirmation or merely letting be. In recent years on both sides of the generation gap, on both extremes of the political spectrum, and on both sides of every militant social and racial confrontation, there has been a tendency to regard some people as totally irrelevant because they are not "where it is at." The "community of otherness" stands in uncompromising opposition to this tendency. We have freedom and we must stand our own ground; but we are not the whole of reality, and we find our true being is going out to meet what is not ourselves. Even if aging people are not the wise sages that T.S. Eliot pretended they were, they are still inalienable members of our community, and we cannot ignore their voices without losing our own humanity.

The building of true community is the building of a community of otherness. It is not requisite upon a community to turn itself inside out for the sake of the old people in its midst. But much depends upon whether it takes action as a real community which listens to the voices of all or just as a majority which is able to override those whose voices are no longer heard at all or are heard and discounted because they are the voices of the aged. Sometimes our dialogue can only mean standing our ground in opposition to the aged; yet it can never mean being unconcerned for how the aged sees the world or careless of the validity of their standing where they do! The reality of community is polyphonic; it is many-voiced. In a community of otherness the voice of the aged is heard because real community creates an atmosphere of trust which enables them to make their witness. I have been in very few groups in my life, including the finest, where real community has not been violated day after day by a few "weighty" persons imposing their will upon the less sure and the less articulate in the name of what should be done. Only a real listening—a listening witness—can plumb the abyss of that universal existential mistrust that stands in the way of the coming to be of a community of otherness.

If we can overcome existential mistrust with candor and the community of affinity with the community of otherness, even as we age, we may be able to begin anew.

> A fiddler once played Rabbi Hanok a tune. He said: "Even melodies that grow old lose their savor. When we heard this one at Rabbi Bunam's long ago, it made our hearts leap. Now it has lost its savor. And that is how it really is. We must be very well prepared and ready for old age. We pray: 'Cast me not off in the time of old age!' For then we lose our savor. But sometimes this is a good thing. For when I see that after all I have done I am nothing at all, I must start my work over again. And it is said of God: 'Who reneweth the creation every day continually'."

It is this beginning anew that I should like to achieve in my own life as I enter old age, and it is this that I hope for and, with this paper, would point to as a realistic hope for the lives of others. Obeying an impulse of the heart, I recently tracked down and wrote to a friend with whom I had not been in touch for forty years, not knowing whether I would get a response at all or if I did what response I might expect. In a few weeks a letter came back which has heartened me enormously in beginning anew. I am sure that my friend too is "not at all young," but she is "old in a young way."

> After all these years, after graduating from the sculpture department at Yale, after showing for the first time at the age of twenty three, after marrying a painter, and after raising three daughters I am now happily divorced and living in New Yortk. I am still a sculptor with twenty-some solo shows and my share of recognition. In January, after thirty years of teaching, I quit to concentrate on being the kind of sculptor I always felt I would be when I could give it my full attention. This is a glorious time for me. I wake up every morning delighted not to have to go to the college. My work is expanding and taking new directions with a great burst of energy.

To be old is a glorious thing if one knows how to begin anew!

FOOTNOTES

[1]Maurice Friedman, *The Hidden Human Image* (New York: Delacorte Press, Delta Books [paperback], 1974), Chap. 9—"Death and the Dialogue with the Absurd," pp. 149-51.

[2]Martin Buber, *Eclipse of God: Studies in the Relation between Religion and Philosophy* (New York: Harper Torchbooks, 1957), "Prelude: Report on Two Talks," trans. by Maurice Friedman, p. 6.

[3]Maurice Friedman, *Touchstones of Reality: Existential Trust and the Community of Peace* (New York: Dutton Books [paperback], 1974, p. 319

[4]Martin Buber, *Tales of the Hasidim: The Early Masters*, trans. by Olga Marx (New York Schocken Books, 1978), p. xii

THE AGING GENIUS

Richard W. Wiseman

Frequently the final works of aging genius are so imbued with secret joys, the great energies of life and the sources of freedom, that the typical faltering of an individual in the last stages of organic being does not obtain. There is a kinship of achievement, transcendence, vibrancy, often noted by critics studying their work. An example from W. Riezler's book on *Beethoven:*

> The second *Oedipus* of Sophocles and Goethe's *Faust Part II* entirely different as they are in externals, have kindred sounds that meet across the millenia. And that it is not merely the octogenarian mind that thus expresses itself is shown by a last work such as Shakespeare's *Tempest* . . . all seem to have their origin in the same world.

Although no one is ever able to ground the distinctive feature of the actual works, ever able to find descriptive adjectives even slightly satisfactory, it is possible to point out some of the realms of the aging genius:

In the last self-portraits of Rembrandt we can observe and speak of the suffused light, the rich tones, the luminosity suggestive of high spiritual qualities, yet often surrounding a roguish smile, an ambiguous yet warm and compassionate twinkle in the eyes; tolerance expressed and the manifest overcoming of great bitterness.

Or, as suggested by the critic struggling to say something lucid about the late works of Beethoven, who feels compelled to turn to other arts to illustrate his point, there is the magic and mystery combined with such earthy, biological concerns in the fanciful world of Shakespeare's *Winters Tale* and *The Tempest*.Or the spacousness and energy of Beethoven's last sonatas and quartets; the seemingly inexhaustible realms of expression in Bach's *Art of Fugue* and *A Musical Offering;* the prototypes of life symbols and images ironically but devotedly and passionately considered in Goethe's *Faust Part II.*

There is literally no stopping when a commentary turns to the delights of these works, but I am committed to exploring the uses of such material quite practically in the regimen of older citizens.

In considering the possibilities of signals from aging genius as therapy for the aging, care should be taken to observe the entire life-achievement pattern: a youthful genius and the typical works of that period, the prime of greatest energy and accomplishment and then the final phase: showing acceptance, not resignation, no time for bitterness and certainly none for discouragement . . . and in this picture the older citizens may well perceive an echo, however remote, coming from the remembered landscape of their own life patterns.

The human race learns and is challenged at every phase of its development by its unusual members—often called geniuses. The youthful, the mature adults are exposed to this demand, this irritating and upsetting measuring-stick. What 17-year-old has not had a jolt when he becomes aware of the extent of Mozart's creativity by that age? What individual in middle life can contemplate with complete equanimity the epoch-making work of Einstein by the time he was 40 or 50 years of age?

But, above all, why not use examples of genius in old

age for those citizens who are also old, use them not for the purpose of discouragement, not as put-down, but clearly as an enhancement of the quality of life. Especially if those aging in our society feel that everything wondrous and important lies behind them, if they seem prone to depression because of the stage of life in which they find themselves—then they are likely to receive a great bolstering from humans who are likewise old, yet who obviously find only in old age creative areas of space and time they could not reach before.

We might well start from Jung's perspective that nature is never truly prodigal or wasteful and yet our species alone continues to live and breathe and respond to stimuli as much as 30 years after the brood, the offsprings, have been tended and launched into their own lives. What is nature's purpose or design for our species with this gift of 30 additonal years of life-time?

I am proposing the usefulness of statements by aging geniuses as preparation for the highest spiritual moments of the aging process. This, despite the fact that there is a theory abroad that only low-keyed, low-calibre material should be seen before any monority group of our society—to avoid causing feelings of inferiority, to avoid accusation of snobbery and I know not what. But geniuses, especially in old age, do not pay attention to such things, even for a moment; their concern is with quality, with depth and energy of expression and never with the pedestrian, shallow, vapid images of life.

A question could be raised about the obvious predilection in this anlysis for artistic genius. Most of my examples are taken from the "exceptional" realm of the artist. However, this is a facet of our age which represents a whole cultural shift and is not unique to the situation of old age. The literature of the portrait of the artist in James Joyce, Thomas Mann, Henry James, Hermann Hesse and even Proust and Romain Rolland is part of our society's symptomatology: the reliable cosmos of a god-given ethic now departed, we can appeal only to our vision of the integrity of the artist, his devotion to quality, which proves to us that he still believes in the worth of human life. Thus the integrity of the artist provides the new imagery of the call of the spirit; our age has found its root of confidence there.

Biographical writings and documentary films enable us to participate in the different levels of the lives of great political figures, great scientists: Madame Curie, Albert Schweitzer and many others. But it is in the constant confessional record of the human condition in great artists to whom it has been vouchsafed to live through all stages of life and creativity that we get probably our most compelling, persuasuve images.

In this connection, I should like to examine a very specific example, showing in what at first may appear to be a very remote and unlikely place, the intimate concern of the aging for the world, their lingering desire to instruct, their compassion, despite their seeming distance and remoteness. At the age of 90, Sophocles worked for one final time with the *Oedipus* legend. It had been with him toward the beginning of his writing career when he composed the *Antigone* and again in the period of full mastery with the famous *Oedipus the King*. Then, at the last he contemplated the final hours in the life of his hero in *Oedipus at Colonus*. Here he gives us what we might desire to call a 90-year-old's lesson in tolerance, as we ponder how a typical group of humans learns from the accursed, blind old irascible beggar, Oedipus:

First, Oedipus is someone to be feared, driven out:

Chorus: Away! Begone! Leave our land.
Oedipus: But your promise. What of your promise!

Then the chorus tries to participate in the grief and anguish of Oedipus. They seek to know:

"of that heartache; the pain you have had to bear."

From the things they then hear and see they are tempted to characterize the fate of Oedipus as the occasion for complete despair:

> It is best never to be born
> But if you are
> Second best is to hasten quickly out of life.

But the aging Sophocles has no intention of leaving them in this unmitigated pessimism. The chorus begins to accept what they perceive in a different fashion:

> Who am I to say: time's purpose falters—
> Fate is moving, changing, turning;
> No decree of the gods is in vain.

And, as the play ends, purified at last in their insights, they know that the story of Oedipus, ultimately, is the motivation of joy rather than despair and they say to the weeping daughters of Oedipus:

> But cease now, and nevermore lift up the lament
> For all these things possess ultimate authority.

Shakespeare's parting message is framed in the utterly different tonality of *The Tempest* and yet we must note that when the beautiful masque collapses, and young Ferdinand is terrified, Prospero says:

Be cheerful, sir. Our revels now are ended

Not, in the final analysis, "... and my ending is despair" rather, as with Sophocles: Nevermore lift up the lament, be cheerful, sir. And these messages from Prospero and Sophocles, how similar they are to the courage of the dying Mozart, who said farewell to the world with *The Magic Flute,* a serious and charming statement, whose basic premise is identical with *The Tempest,* a fact almost always missed by the commentators. How did Mozart come into the ranks of the aging genius? I find it always useful to remember the remark of a collegue of mine: "Mozart was 55 years old when he was born."

Mozart's Prospero is called Sarastro in *The Magic Flute*. He arranges for the testing of the young lovers, just as his counterpart did in *The Tempest*; he looks with a wry smile but without bitterness at the foibles of his fellow creatures. And if Pamina had exclaimed: "O brave new world, that hath such creatures in it." He would surely have replied: "Tis new to thee." Mozart's valediction is a work that can utterly delight a child and at the same time obsess the most complex and imaginative human sensibility; we recall that Goethe was so fascinated with what Mozart had done, he tried to write a sequel, parts of which, incidentally, found their appropriate way into *Faust Part II*.

In a more practical vein: what we have been sketching here is the possibility of living creatively, even the creativity of living differently. Anyone in contact with these true radicals of old age can have no chance to learn the clichés of aging in our society; there is no chance to relegate them to the old-folks home of the mind. Inspired by Shakespeare, let us say, whenever older citizens are in the presence of confused and frightened youth, they can come forward with their own equivalent of 'be cheerful sir.' They may be rewarded with a strange smile, even with a tentative rejection. But they can feel that young person has caught some faint glimpse of a special kind of courage, combined with acceptance, at the end of life's journey, and this kind of encounter may have important consequences for the other soul's recovery from cynicism and negativity.

I am saying that the more our senior citizens feel the importance of their stage of life, the more they have these inspirations of genuine depth and authenticity to convince them, the more they will be able to show forth, in a thousand different daily ways, the wisdom we justly expect from them. They can let us grow in their presence as the chorus in *Oedipus at Colonus* grows in the presence of Oedipus—from *our* state of fear and rejection to our way of accepting the human condition.

And this is a gift of love and courage from one human being to another which ignores boundaries of race or sex or age—it knows no generation gap. Nor does it have to await that re-training into more perceptive awareness of our obligations toward the old age of ourselves, our neighbors, our society—while that essential work is being argued and tentatively, experimentally begun, *this* human gesture can go daily forward, rewarding both giver and receiver.

Perhaps it all has something to do with Yeats' extravagant phrasing:

> Through all the lying days of youth
> I waved my leaves and flowers in the sun.
> Perhaps now I may wither
> Into the truth.

Think, in this regard, of Jane Austen who wrote novel after novel about the lie of her life, her dear, dear sisters, her sympathetic father, her fascinating suitor, always out of reach. Then at the very end, in *Persuasion*, she had the courage to tell the real story: the sisters were gossips, the father a kind of negligent monster, the suitor she had pinned all those dreams on was actually a fatuous ass.

We can also be reminded here of the pianist Lili Kraus who insists that her devastating experiences in a Japanese prison camp during World War II were her catalyst, the passageway to her artistic achievements in her final years as a performing artist. And that strange phenomenon of the Victorian era, Mrs. Bird Bishop, the paragon of precision and propriety, who found her catalyst in a blizzard one night in the mountains of China. Her journal of her travels changes after that experience, the statistics are gone, and in a startling chapter called *The Beyond* she writes of her appreciation of the beauty of the earth planet. Her brush with death cleansed away all the lies and pretence: "land brighter than youth, its beauty left nothing to be longed for."

I know not what blizzard or prison camp each wise older citizen must pass through. In Thoman Mann's *The Magic Mountain* the key to transformation of the human soul is likewise told in the imagery of a mountain blizzard. And Mann freed his hero thus, and himself, into the roguish possibilities of *Felix Krull,* where all former doubts and sophistries are dissolved in an irresistable stream of life and love. And the motives of generosity and forebearance in Solzhenitsyn's Nobel Prize Speech stem from his own unimaginable experiences with the world of the prison camp.

I am talking about cognition through images, intense human images in sculpture, poetry, music, painting: recognizable landscapes of the soul. I am talking about fortitude and thoughts that lie too deep for tears, about ceaseless experiment, work, boldness, greater demands, breadth, freedom. Whatever can be grasped of this by any age group is worth all risks, it is a rigorous lure for any individual, any life community.

Perhaps I can show more forcefully how clear and simple my premise really is by evoking Hugo von Hofmannsthal's brilliant intuition about aging genius in his play, *The Death of Titian.*

It is a gorgeious late afternoon in Venice. Titian, the master, lies dying while his disciples and pupils foregather on the terrace of his villa as the sunset sky changes from livid reds and purples to a pulsating mother-of-pearl. They converse languidly and knowledgeably about the tragic and depressing aspects of the great painter's death: no one has understood his work, the public knows nothing, really, of his use of color, his growing passion in the designs and inter-relationships on each canvas, the unimaginable subtlety and strength of his last paintings. And so on and on. Finally, someone decides to go inside and inquire after

Titian himself, perhaps to say a word or two to mollify him, to assuage the great sorrow and disappointment which must surely be tormenting him and darkening his final hours . . .

The messenger returns with a dazed expression. Titian has gotten up from his bed, crossed the room to his easel and , during these last hours which his pupils have wasted on vain lamentation, he has been working, working furiously and devotedly-courageously, existentially, doing what must be done.

And this is certainly not an isolated event, invented by a young playwright sentimentally in love with his projections onto old age. It is known that the feverish Michelangelo, five days before his death, almost 90 years of age, on February 18, 1564, was working on a radical new vision as he altered completely the Rondanini Pieta. We know that Mozart worked on the *Requiem* on his death bed and that he always looked at his watch in the evening in order to participate in imagination and with unwavering delight in the performance of *Magic Flute* going forward each evening at the *Theater an der Wien*.

With film and videotape, these kinds of things are much more available now than at any previous time. There are interviews: Julie Harris talking to the very old Eva Le Gallienne; there is a fine videotape of Lili Kraus performing and talking about her key life experiences. There is Rudolf Serkin playing so splendidly in Carnegie Hall, prayerfully folding his hands when Beethoven doesn't have anything for him to do at a given moment. Or there is Sir Thomas Beecham at eighty, conducting the superb Chicago Symphony in Berlioz, visibly murmuring 'Give 'em hell, brass.' There is Georgia O'Keefe walking about the New Mexico desert, looking for the object whose purity of form will speak to her and cause her to surpass herself in a new painting of even greater severity and control. Or there is Martha Graham, talking to the discouraged young dancer, who wants to retreat, who fears she can never measure up to the high standards of her teacher: encouraging her with the simple words: 'Only you can do your dances now.'

Once again, what has emerged here, in this contemplation of unusual humans in old age that can contribute to new perspectives on aging?

In the last messages we have noted elements of humor, mystery, spaciousness, joyous acceptance, freedom. And to sum it all up, it might be best to stress that last attribute, since it is most likely just the factor which the average older citizens feel they have forfeited. In growing old they have lost their most precious possession, their freedom. But the aging geniuses show clearly that this is not the case. They have freedom to *be* only at the last—all the hampering commitments are gone - and they can touch pure, un-hampered, unobstructed existence. The role-playing is over, the surface-level obligations are largely over, and they are nothing more and nothing less than human.

In one of his last poems, the last of the *Sonnets to Orpheus*, Rilke puts it:

> From what experience have you suffered most?
> Is drinking bitter?
> Become wine!

Rembrandt's youthful self-portraits show a typical human vanity: see how the light of earth and sky reveals my jaunty fur-cap and the Belgian lace on my collar—see how dashing, mysterious and interesting I am! But in the final portraits we can see a reversal of the function of light as radical as Rilke's strange poetic injunction. No longer does the light exist in order to reveal the fascinating human presence, but we sense that old battered face, those smudges of paint, that revelation utterly cleansed of vanity, exist simply to bring into being that rich ivory light. Thus, we have a chance to learn that even a very old face, seemingly devoid of any beauty, is the possibility of light.

Perhaps a lecture-presentation of the amazing self-portraits of Rembrandt will reach *your* group of aging citizens best. Or the last sculptures of Michelangelo, or the last messages of Leonardo da Vinci—if you find music or poetry not speaking so clearly. Even so, you will find the pathway for them. Try Walt Whitman on Americans. From the utterly earthy practicality of the usual Whitman, take them to the late metaphysical wonder of *Passage to India*. Try then to read to them his valedictory, *Goodbye my Fancy*, without perceiving some tears of happiness.

Or perhaps living, moving pictures of re-creative genius will have a more immediate effect: Rudolf Serkin, or Horowitz or Rubinstein—very old, often cantankerous but mainly calm and radiant, full of energy and prayer, praying to their god of artistic integrity; absolute, definitive devotion to the task. And the energy and fire, the noble strength of great conductors: Bruno Walter and Beecham and Toscanini and Furtwangler. Pierre Monteux near 90. Performers of all the arts: jazz, blues, vaudeville, films: Sir Laurence Olivier.

The aging genius usually has no time for regrets. The last phase, old age, is the beginning, the country they always wanted to reach. Now they can be Felix Krull, the rouge, the trickster, Hermes - the imbuing of matter with unthinkable energy - the real meaning of life.

YOUR OLD MEN SHALL DREAM DREAMS

Christine Downing

> A human being would certainly not grow to be seventy
> or eighty years old if this longevity had no meaning for
> the species. The afternoon of life must also have sig-
> nificance of its own and cannot be merely a pitiful
> appendage of life's morning.[1]

These words of Carl Jung invite us to consider the creative process in relation to the image of the wise old man and not only as we usually do in relation to the child. So often we identify the creative with characteristics associated with youth—originality, spontaneity, play, narcissism—and ignore the *work* of art, the discipline, the ordering, the recognition of limits. All our tribute is given Dionysos or Eros; we forget the sacrifice due Apollo and death. Even when we recognize the conjunction of creativity and death, we may well have in mind the "romantic" premature death of a Keats or a Novalis. "He whom the gods love dies young," we say. But death, too, is viewed differently from the perspective of the morning of life than from its afternoon. Perhaps there are insights about the creative process, about what sustains it and brings it to maturity and not only about what gives it birth, to be gained from the contemplation of the late works of those writers who do grow to be seventy or eighty years old.

This would be especially true of late works consciously understood by their creators as part of their own preparation for death and as in some sense works of self-completion, works in which old man and youth are rejoined. Thus last works which are obviously completions of projects begun much earlier are of particular interest. Though I intend here to focus on Sophocles' *Oedipus at Colonus* and Thoman Mann's *Felix Krull*, the most obvious example of such a last work is probably Goethe's *Faust*, of which Mann wrote:

> A life so abundant and manifold that there was ever present danger of its being squandered, here asserts, by the power of memory, its essential unity. *Faust* is the representative achievement, the symbol of Goethe's whole life. He himself said of it:
> Man's life a poem similar to this;
> It has, of course, beginning, has an end too—
> But yet a whole life it does not come to.
> It is touching to see how his mind, in the later, elder, time, reaches back to give to the fragmentary and illimitable work the unity that in his deepest heart he craved. "He is," he said, "the most fortunate man who can bring the end of his life round to its beginning again."[2]

In his study of Leonardo da Vinci, Sigmund Freud suggests such a reunion of *senex* and *puer* as integral to the creativity of the mature. He believes that when the aging artist's creativity was waning, it was through regression to his infantile experience, with "the help of his oldest erotic energies," that he found renewal. The mysterious smile of the Mona Lisa inspired Leonardo because it awakened in him the earliest memories of his mother.

Mann seems to invoke this presentation of Leonardo as prototype of the artist renewed by contact with youth in several of his own "studies" of the artist. Mona Lisa's smile may well lie behind the enigmatic smile of Tadzio which stirs Mann's aging artist, Gustave Aschenbach, in *Death in Venice*, written shortly after Freud's study. Is not Felix Krull's becoming Louis de Venosta (L. d. V.), sketchpad in hand, a not too subtle indication of Mann's recognition, when *he* has become the aging artist, of his bond with Freud's Leonardo—a bond mediated through his youthful protagonist Felix, who is also thus "the fortunate man" whom Goethe described?

Such connections seem legitimate because Mann has made explicit acknowledgement of his indebtedness to Freud, his conviction that Freud, particularly in his late works (the works from the time of *Leonardo* and *Totem and Taboo* onward), points the way to "a relation to the powers of the lower world, the unconscious... productive of a riper art."[3] In these metapsychological works in which Freud self-confessedly returns to his long-neglected philosophical interests, to "the early passion of his youth," he offers us a psychology particularly appropriate to the second half of life, as his earlier more therapeutically-oriented works pertain primarily to the concerns of the young: work and love. In the later writings Freud recognizes the coming to terms with death as the central task of life and posits the discovery of the mythopoeic dimensions of our lives as an essential part of this preparation.

The beautiful essay written by Mann in celebration of Freud's eightieth birthday indicates that the reconnection with the past which inspires the mature artist is not just a recovery of personal infancy and youth but "a penetration into the childhood of mankind, into the primitive and mythical." For, "while in the life of the human race, the mythical is an early and primitive stage, in the life of the individual it is a late and mature one." Mann speaks of the "curious heightening of his artist temper," the "new refreshment of his perceiving and shaping power," that comes when an artist acquires "the habit of regarding life as mythical and typical." He relates this to the transition in his own career (which he identifies with the beginning of the *Joseph* cycle) from "the bourgeois and individual to the mythical and typical."[4]

Freud, so Mann tells us, helps us to understand what it means for myth to "become subjective," to pass over into "the active ego, becoming conscious there proudly and darkly, but joyously of its recurrence and typicality."[5] For Freud maturity means becoming conscious of our participation in mythic patterns and thus discovering a kind of freedom in relation to them. This is the significance of his putting the working-through of the transference at the center of the psychoanalytical process. For when we come to understand the degree to which all our experiencing is the reliving of ancient patterns and to recognize how much we shape our present on the basis of imaginal (not literal) versions of our past, we can become aware of the symbolic and thus make the move from repetition to recognition, from myth to mythopoesis.

The move to mythopoesis is also a move beyond the monomyth of the hero; the heroic illusion persists only as long as one is still caught in the identification of the ego with the myth. That identification represents what Jung calls "inflation:" taking the myth literally, not yet recognizing myth as myth. As we transcend the confusion of the literal and the symbolic, we become conscious of the multidimensionality of what happens between us and the others intimately implicated in our lives and learn to celebrate our capacity to transfer onto those we love our deepest longings—knowing exactly what we are up to. Mann calls what is gained "a smiling knowledge of the eternal," a release from bondage to the identification of the real with the unique and unitemporal. Freud suggests that the capacity to distinguish between the literal and the symbolic is integrally related to our conversion to finitude, our acceptance of Ananke and Death. Trying to repress myth, like Oedipus trying to evade the oracle, is what gets us into trouble, but participating in the myth knowingly is utterly different from unknowing compulsion. Thus the cultivation of mythic consciousness becomes the primary challenge of old age.

We might expect then that in the artistic works of old men we might find evidence of this more subjective, more conscious relation to myth. It is not so much the presence of mythical themes that distinguishes youth from maturity as a different relation to myth. There is more freedom for creative response to the inherited patterns rather than simple determination by them, more awareness that we are implicated in a plurality of myths and not wholly defined by any one, and that our participation in mythic patterns is not just a matter of seemingly accidental and superficial parallels but of the basic structures of our being. Mann's conviction that the move to this deeper appreciation of the mythical characterizes the mature artist suggests that when Sophocles returns to Oedipus after a twenty year lapse, when he himself returns to *Felix Krull* after an interval almost twice as long, we might look for a different approach to the same material—both the return to the beginning which Goethe commends and the transformation which *Faust II* exemplifies.

Thus we should not be surprised if the Oedipus of *Oedipus at Colonus* the Krull of Parts II and III, are more aware and more accepting of their participation in mythic patterns than was true of them in their earlier appearances. The mythopoetic logic of the psyche which Freud articulated in his later years suggests some other themes we might look for in literary works written by those engaged in coming to terms with age and death. Whereas in youth the heroic stance is appropriate, in later years the overcoming of egoic illusions, the recognition that life is *poesis* and *pathos,* doing and suffering inextricably intertwined, is crucial. Thus the focus shifts from the quest of the hero to the battle between the Titans, Eros and Death. And with the yielding of the heroic there comes an end to the exaltation of the tragic; in its place there appears the recognition (long ago voiced by Socrates at the end of the *Symposium*) that the tragic and comic visions do not exclude one another. The more mature relation to myth means not only the transcendence of the heroic but also the end of the hypermasculinity so often correlative with it. In *Analysis Terminable and Interminable* Freud suggests that the overcoming of misogyny, the subversion of our repudiation of our feminity (be we men or women) is the most difficult task of analysis. The full acceptance of self includes the discovery of our psychological bisexuality, in mythological terms of our hermaphroditism. The new perspective also implies release from the hero's mother complex, from his seeking everywhere for a reanimation of his literal mother and from his obsessive longing for rebirth, his nostalgia for innocence. It is now understood that the realm of the mother means death as well as rebirth, that mother means tomb and not only womb. In his essay on "The Three Caskets" Freud speaks of

> the three forms taken on by the figure of the mother as life proceeds: the mother herself, the beloved who is chosen after her pattern, and finally the Mother Earth who receives him again. But it is in vain that the old man yearns after the love of woman as once he had it from his mother; the third of the Fates, alone, the silent goddess of death will take him into her arms.[6]

He shows how Cordelia's death means that King Lear must now renounce love, choose death and make friends with the necessity of dying. Paradoxically, the radical acceptance of death entails the realization that it does not mean the end, does not mean resolution or completion. There are no tidy ends; in Freud's terms, analysis is interminable.

Send Us Back Then To Ancient Thebes

Even at the time of *Interpretation of Dreams* Oedipus meant to Freud not only patricide and incest but the long and painful process of self-discovery. This myth represented the pull each of us experiences toward being our own father, toward denying our separation from our mother, and the recognition that we cannot get away with either. "Resolution" of the Oedipus complex entails the move toward a different kind of seeing, toward transliteral, sacred understanding. Freud understands the significance of the fact that in *Oedipus Rex* only the blind see; literal blindness, blindness to the literal, makes possible imaginal, metaphorical perception. But some twenty years later Freud, now painfully cancer-ridden, recognized even more profoundly that the story of Oedipus does not end in Jocasta's bed but in Demeter's grove outside of Athens. As throughout his years of wandering Oedipus' eyes were his daughter, Antigone, so now Sigmund's mouth is his daughter, "my Anna/Antigone." There is more to being Oedipus than at first appears. Freud had discovered early: I am Oedipus; you, too, are Oedipus. As his longing and guilt are ours, so, Freud seems now to suggest, *could* be his death, "wonderful if ever mortal's was."

When Sophocles returns to Oedipus some twenty years after the composition of *Oedipus Rex*, he portrays Oedipus as dying at Colonus, his own birthplace. Thus he conveys that this, his last play (which he probably did not live to see performed), represents a homecoming. Although this is not sheer invention on Sophocles' part (there were ancient Attic traditions in its support, our familiarity with Sophocles' version may blind us to how much more freely Sophocles has reworked received version of the myth in the *Colonus* than in the earlier play. There are widely varying accounts of what happens to Oedipus after his downfall. The most popular seems to have said nothing of banishment at all: Oedipus was simply shut up in an inner room of the palace at Thebes. According to Homer he dies in battle at Thebes as befits a hero. Another ancient tradition has him exiled and after years of aimless wandering dying in the wild wastelands near the place where he slew Laius. In Euripides' *The Phoenician Women* Oedipus, long a prisoner in Thebes, does not leave the city until after he has witnessed the horrifying fulfillment of his curse: his sons have slain one another and only after witnessing that has Jocasta in her grief killed herself. In Apollodorus as in

Sophocles, Oedipus dies at Colonus, but whereas according to Sophocles,[6] "the underworld opened in love the unlit door of earth," according to Apollodorus he is hounded to death by the Furies.

It is clear that Sophocles felt free consciously to rework the story in the light of his own vision of a death appropriate to an Oedipus who has lived long enough to understand the meaning of his own story. The more conscious relation to myth is thus also reflected in the protagonist's own self-understanding. The Oedipus of the *Coloneus* is aware that he is living a myth, is a living myth. As the chorus tells him, "Old man, your name has gone over all the earth" (305); Your story "is told everywhere and never dies: I only want to hear it truly told" (517,8). Oedipus himself has come to recognize how all of his life has been lived in accordance with the oracle. Trying to evade living out the mythic pattern only intensified its power over him:

> The bloody deaths, the incest, the calamities
> You speak so glibly of: I suffered them,
> By fate, against my will. (962-4)

But he trusts that the rest of Apollo's prophecy is also to be fulfilled, and soon:

> For when he gave me oracles of evil,
> He also spoke of this: A resting place,
> After long years, in the last country, where
> I should find home among the sacred Furies:
> That there I might round out my bitter life,
> Conferring benefit on those who received me. (87-92)

The blind Oedipus who has come to Colonus has now himself become the possessor of that clairvoyant insight which earlier (because he could not bear to see) had been carried by Tiresias. Oedipus has now become Tiresias in another sense as well. Though Tiresias remains the only mortal to have experienced life both as male and female,

Oedipus, in a less literal sense has during his years of exile lived as a woman. His blindness is a kind of castration; he has had to come to terms with a dependent status conventionally associated with the feminine, has had to surrender the heroic masculine notion of being able to make the world conform to his wishes He has also learned how little gender determines our psychological orientation and how multiple are the confusions of object-love and identification-love in any primary relationship. He recognizes that Antigone who is not only his daughter but also his sister is also at times his son. She and Ismene "are not girls but men in faithfulness" (1368), while their brothers" sit by the fire like home-loving girls" (342).

Oedipus in this final scene of his life re-enacts the mythic pattern which is so indelibly associated with his name. He is still Oedipus—and yet, because he understands now what he is about, the meaning is utterly different. His readiness to enter the forbidden grove of Demeter is a repetition of his earlier readiness to enter the forbidden womb of Jocasta. But now (as Slochower has noted)[7] there is this crucial difference: "This return to the mother takes place, not on a literal, but on a *symbolic* level." Oedipus has learned now that literal incest is beside the point.

The importance of the recognition that the return to the mother is to be enacted symbolically is a major theme in the writings of Carl Jung. This theme is boldly articulated in *Symbols of Transformation*, the work which both he and Freud understood as a consciously patricidal attempt to free himself from domination by Freud and establish his own unmediated relation to the unconscious. Jung found Freud's understanding of incest too literal and too biological; he was persuaded that incest longing, properly understood, is always symbolical. It represents the longing for spiritual rebirth, for renewal at the source of life. The forbidding of literal incest, the taboo, forces the move toward symbolization and spiritual transformation. The point of regression is introversion, the relation not to the parents but to the collective psyche. The prohibition (or in Oedipus' case, the punishment of its violation) forces further regression to the mother as nourisher and not as sexual object. Thus it is his blindness which represents the introversion that brings Oedipus to the Demetrian grove.

The pull toward the mother and the taboo which says, not the literal mother, not literal sex, moves us toward spiritual transformation. Jung's interpretation suggests the necessity of the kind of symbolic incest which Oedipus commits at Colonus. "The fear of incest must be conquered," the hero is the one who yields to the incest wish.[8]

> Therapy must support the regression and continue to do so until the "pre-natal" stage is reached . . . The regression leads back only apparently to the mother; in reality she is the gateway into the unconscious, into the "realm of the Mother."[9]

(It seems pertinent that in the preface to this book Jung should acknowledge his identification with Theseus. He is to Theseus as Freud is to Oedipus. Theseus' daring of the labyrinth is the equivalent in his life of Oedipus' entry into the grove, but at a much earlier point in his life. At Colonus it is Theseus who is the only one present to witness Oedipus' descent and to whom Oedipus' secret is passed on: an image clearly consonant with Jung's understanding of his relation to Freud.)

At Colonus Oedipus' return to the mother is symbolic, and cognizant of the mother in her role as the silent goddess of death. Having in the violent act of self-blinding had a preliminary experience of death as Thanatos defines it, Oedipus is now ready for death as it is understood in Demeter's realm. Here death means reunion with Persephone ("Veled Persephone lead me on" 1548); death is now blessing not curse, initiation not termination. This death is a kind of introduction into the Eleusinian mysteries of which Sophocles said elsewhere: "Thrice happy are those of mortals, who having seen these rites depart for Hades; for to them alone is it granted to have found life there; to the rest all there is evil."[10]

At Colonus everything is turned around. What had been a source of difficulty has become a blessing to be celebrated. The grove is a place of many reversals and transformations. The gods have not forgiven Oedipus nor has he been brought to accept his sinfulness.[11] But he has suffered long enough to have come to accept his life as it has been without trying any longer to argue a distinction between "so it was" and "so I willed it."[12] The years of wandering serve as the equivalent of participation in the preparatory outwardly visible phases of the Eleusinian initiation. The burial place of one whose presence during the years of exile had been perceived as curse will be a source of blessing. The Furies who haunt violators of the mother so mercilessly now appear as the Eumenides, "the gentle all-seeing ones." Blind Oedipus long led by Antigone now becomes the guide.

These resolutions do not depend on Oedipus' story now being explained; the mystery which has surrounded his life is not dissolved:

> Now the finish
> Comes, and we know only
> In all that we have seen and done
> Bewildering mystery. (1675-8)

The lines describing Oedipus' end are utterly beautiful:

> But in what manner
> Oedipus perished, no one of mortal men
> Could tell but Theseus. It was not lightning,
> Bearing its fire from God, that took him off;
> No hurricane was blowing.
> But some attendant from the train of Heaven
> Came for him: or else the underworld
> Opened in love the unlit door of earth.
> For he was taken without lamentation,

Illness or suffering: indeed his end
Was wonderful if ever mortal's was. (1655-65)

Yet this wonderful end does not betoken the end of human tragedy. Sophocles does not offer us a world which after Oedipus' death is restored to harmony. The last lines of the play communicate a vision of the interminable quality of the troubledness of human existence. The curse Oedipus visited upon his sons is still to be fulfilled; Antigone and Ismene, grief-shattered, confront a "wide and desolate world," with no way clear before them.

Nevertheless in his last tragedy Sophocles offers us his vision of a wonder-full, creature death—a death in which a "bitter life" is transformed into something that "confers benefit."

Holé Heho, Ahé

As Sophocles returned in his last tragedy to a figure whose story he had begun to relate some twenty years earlier, so Thomas Mann returned at the end of his life to continuing the narration of the adventures of a character who had made his first appearance more than forty years earlier. Mann began "Felix Krull" in 1910 and already guessed then, "It will probably be my strangest work."[13] He put it aside, so he thought temporarily, to work on "Death in Venice," and then published the completed fragment in 1912, having discovered that he was not ready to take it further after all. He came to regard it as a youthful expression, "belonging to an outmoded bourgeois-artist period" in his history as a writer. This phase of Mann's life is perhaps comparable to the one in Freud's during which he wrote his case histories. After World War I both Freud and Mann had moved to a view of life so deeply attuned to the shaping power of mythic forces on individual existence that the earlier focus on individual quest no longer seemed an appropriate vehicle. "Felix" seemed to belong to that outgrown period.

Yet in late 1945 after finishing the *Joseph* cycle, Mann found himself picking up the fragment again, as though there were after all something to be finished here. He had an intuition that the completion of "Felix Krull" might in some way be meant to be his last work. Again another project became more immediately compelling and Mann soon found himself completely immersed in the writing of *Dr. Faustus*. But then in 1950 he returned to "Felix", still uncertainly ("perhaps it will only be mischief"), and on this occasion found it was indeed time to take up the old tale once again. It was finished in 1954 and was, after all, his last work.

The return to "Krull" is continuation—and transformation. As Mann wrote Carl Kerenyi:

> I was not aware, God knows, of undertaking a Hermetic novel when I began with this forty years ago. I had no other intention than yet another impersonation and parody of art and the artist. It was only in the course of the subsequent continuation that certain associations, undoubtedly induced by the proximity of the *Joseph*, found their way in, and the name of the god arose.[14]

It is an important part of Krull's acceptance of himself as a confidence man that his trickery brings joy not harm. The recognition of the identity between blessor and violator lies at the heart of *Felix Krull* in its final version and is central to Mann's identification with Felix as archetypal artist: creator and thief in one. (Perhaps *Oedipus at Colonus* is also a hermetic work in Mann's sense. Certainly Oedipus invokes Hermes as well as Persephone to guide him to his death, and the reversals whereby the violator becomes the bringer of blessings have a decidedly hermetic flavor.)

Mann has in the later parts come to see *Krull* in mythic terms not consciously included in his earlier conception. He writes of his delight that once again as so often before he and Kerenyi should have been engaged quite innocently in

such parallel projects; he on his "hermetic novel" and
Kerenyi on the trickster figure in mythology. Of course, a
mythological element is visible in Mann's fiction long before
Joseph. The difference between earlier works, like the beginning of "Krull" and "Death in Venice," and the final
parts of *Krull* is not that myth is present in the latter and
absent from the first but rather in *how* myth is present.
Aschenbach is destroyed through being posessed by the
mythic, taken over by one mythic pattern and not having
any creative freedom in relation to it. Whereas Felix, "favored by fortune," is like Mann's Joseph aware of the many
mythic roles in which he participates. Therefore he can
celebrate the mythic as source of rebirth rather than destruction. He takes delight in his many impersonations,
sees them as providing the means for "renewal of my
worn-out self."[15] He believes that it is the attitude which
underlies one's performances that gives one's activities their
meaning: "For my part I am in agreement with folk wisdom
which holds that when two people do the same it is no
longer the same"(p. 112). It is his ability to see his life as an
artistic creation, in symbolic terms, that underlies his self-
enjoyment. His spurning of Strathbogie's adoption offer
expresses his rejection of "a reality simply handed me" (p.
215). He can take as much delight in passing as less than he
is when he is a waiter as in passing for a marquis. He gives
voice to his most deeply held conviction when he say, "to be
allowed to live symbolically spells true freedom" (p. 101).
As befits one thus attuned to the mythic aspect, he knows
how impossible it would be to disentangle the "good luck"
in his life from his own contribution.

Felix adopts an artistic, mythopoetic attitude toward
life without, however, being consciously informed about
the particular classical mythological roles which he is re-
enacting. He is quick to appreciate the pertinence of the
Hellenic motif when another suggests it, as when Diane
Philibert calls him a Hermes figure, but in large measure the
explicit parallels are conveyed to the reader indirectly. They

are not part of Felix's conscious self-understanding. Thus when Louis asks him," 'Are you strong on mythology?' ", Felix answers, " 'Not very, marquis. There is, for instance, the god Hermes. But aside from him I know very little' " (p. 230).

Yet Felix, as we come to recognize, participates in many myths. Though he might not be able to name his classical counterparts, we see him not only as Hermes but also as Adonis, Actaeon, Eros, and Proteus. Felix's own way of explaining this polymorphism is to say, "He who really loves the world shapes himself to please it" (p. 61).

The Hermes identification is, nevertheless, the central one; not only because Felix as confidence man is Hermes as trickster nor because Felix as waiter is Hermes as servant, but because of Hermes' primal connection with Aphrodite and thus with the image of the hermaphrodite. Much is made in the novel of Krull's slender and delicate beauty and of his being one with whom both men and women fall in love. His own eroticism has a definitely feminine aspect, particularly in its pronouncedly passive orientation. He speaks of "eccentrics who were seeking neither a woman nor a man but some extraordinary being in between. And I was this extraordinary being" (p. 104). And he himself feels the pull toward what he calls a "double creature:" the brother/sister pair on the balcony of the Frankfurt hotel, Andromache the very masculinized female acrobat who arouses his worship.

But Felix's "penchant for twofold enthusiasms" (p. 281), is particularly evident in his attraction to mother/daughter combinations, beginning with his own mother and his sister, Olympia, in the Rhine valley town of his childhood years and ending with Senhora Kuckuck and her daughter, Zouzou, in Lisbon. Though the story of Felix's encounter with the latter pair is comically and joyfully told and has none of the awesome power of Sophocles' drama, here too the climax takes place in "Demeter's grove," that is, in the garden of the Senhora's house. Here, too, Krull is bought to recognize that it is in vain that he turns to the female who most directly arouses his sensual interest, the virginal daughter. For suddenly there stands her mother.

> And yet I ask you to believe that I was less cast down by this maternal apparition than one might have thought. However unexpected her appearance, it seemed fitting and necessary, as though she had been summoned, and in my natural confusion there was an element of joy. (p. 376)

Both Felix and the Senhora recognize that she has come to lead him "back to the right path." It is time for him to encounter "the graciousness of maturity." He had turned to the mortal daughter when he should have turned toward the archetypal mother. As his coming to Lisbon represented his discovery of an "older geological strata in the earth's history" so the Senhora appears to initiate him into primordial, mythical mysteries. He had recognized from the beginning that she was not one to be trifled with. The preceding scene during which Felix becomes aware of the connection between the Senhora's surging bosom and the violence of the bullfight below had made fully manifest the bond between the Mother and death. Now as the novel ends, Felix is aware of "a whirlwind of primordial forces" bearing him "into the realm of ecstasy." Again he sees "the surging of that queenly bosom." The Senhora is clearly the Great Mother and, as Jung says, the hero is the one courageous enough to commit incest.

Perhaps an entirely just appreciation of Mann's own last "confessions" would demand our looking at both *Dr. Faustus* and *Felix Krull* - together they represent a profound honoring of the tragic and comic perspectives on human sufferings. But, that of the two, *Krull* should be the very last seems highly appropriate. Mann in his own old age deliberately chooses Felix, an archetypal *puer aeternus,* to represent artistic creativity, yet without romanticizing the playful and narcissistic aspects of the creative. Felix is well aware that his career is "based on imagination and self-discipline," and that the "great joy," the experience of love given and received is what redeems his trickeries. Because of Felix's youth his turn to DonaMaria is inevitably ambiguous. Is he still caught in a too-literal pull toward the mother or is he, indeed, aware that in turning to the Senhora he is moving into the transformative realm of the Mothers? That ambiguity is, I believe, intentional. Mann does not want to dissolve the mystery of the discovery of the mythical within the actual. And after all, we are by no means at the end of Felix's adventures.

The novel ends—and yet what we have are still only fragments of Felix's confessions. They could theoretically continue interminably. We know that much else is to follow; that at some point in the future, for example, Felix will find himself in prison. Accepting these fragments as all we have is accepting the finitude of life—and recognizing that our fragments nevertheless serve as symbols of wholeness.

Consent to mortality and celebration of the mythical are profoundly intertwined in both *Oedipus at Colonus* and *Felix Krull.* Through this conjuntion, Mann and Sophocles in their last works communicate their "smiling knowledge of the eternal".

San Diego State University
San Diego, California

FOOTNOTES

1. C.G. Jung, "The Stages of life," in Joseph Campbell, editor, *The Portable Jung,* New York: Viking, 1971, p. 17.

2. Thomas Mann, "Goethe's *Faust,"* *Essays of Three Decades,* New York: Alfred A. Knopf, 1971, p. 19.

3. Thomas Mann, "Freud and the Future," *Essays,* New York: Vintage, 1957, p. 323.

4. *Ibid.,* p. 317.

5. *Ibid.,* p. 318.

6. Sophocles, "oedipus at Colonus," in David Grene and Richard Lattimore, editors, *The Complete Greek Tragedies, Volume II,* p. 150. (hereafter line references in test.)

7. Harry Slochower, *Mythopoesis,* Detroit, Wayne State University Press, 1970, p. 90.

8. C.G. Jung, *Symbols Of Transformation,* New York: Pantheon, 1956, p. 294.

9. *Ibid.,* p. 329.

10. Quoted in George E. Mylonas, *Elesis: The Eleusinian Mysteries,* Princeton: Princeton University Press, 1974, p. 284.

11. Cr. H.D. Kitto, *Greek Tragedy,* New York: Doubleday, 1954, p. 419. Nietzsche's definition of redemption.

12. Cf. H.D. Kitto, *Greek Tragedy,* New York: Doubleday, 1954, p. 419. Nietzsche's definition of redemption.

13. Hans Burgin and Hans-Otto Mayer, *Thomas Mann: A Chronicle of His Life,* Alabama: University of Alabama, 1969.

14. Alexander Gelley, translator, *Mythology and Humanism: The Correspondence of Thomas Mann and Karl Kerenyi,* Ithaca: Cornell University Press, 1975, p. 210.

15. Thomas Mann, *Confessions of Felix Krull,* New York: Vintage, 1969, p. 252. Hereafter page references in text.

Death and the Contunity of Life

THE LAST YEARS: Life and Death*

Margaret Frings Keyes

" . . . as we age we are more alive than seems likely, convenient or even bearable . . . It can feel as though all our lives we have been caught in absurdly small personalities and circumstances and beliefs. Our accustomed shell cracks here, cracks there and that tiresomely rigid person we supposed to be ourselves stretches, expands and with all inhibitions gone we realize that age is not failure, not disgrace; though mortifying, we did not invent it. Age forces us to deal with idleness, emptiness, not being needed, not able to do, . . . Now that I am sure that this freedom is the right garnering of age, I am so busy being old that I dread interruptions."
Florida Scott-Maxwell, 83

Each individual man and woman must face for himself/ herself old age with its body difficulties and necessary adjustments. The cultivation of the inner life is recognized as the specific task of the old in most cultures but few of us can accept that idleness, physical pain, emptiness, not being needed, and not being able to do is a necessary condition for bringing to birth a spiritual creation no less important than the creations of earlier periods. We are told that only after the strenuous period of youth and living mid-life to the utmost can the individual acquire wisdom of the inner life through which the whole meaning of his existence can be realized.

Over and over in our lives we experience mini-death blow to our ego and its ambitions, its wantings. We even recognize that some of the times of our greatest growth have come from the devastation and from what we learned and did as a consequence. Life has a way of shoving our nose into what we have to work at until we deal with it. But still we feel with the Spanish philosopher Miguel de Unamuno that old age and death are an insult, an unavoidable fate which should never be considered a just one.

What actually happens in the aging body, the aging psyche, and does it have anything to do with the earlier death/rebirth experiences in our lives? The body demands more and more attention if one is to keep well. Small physical ailments must be taken more seriously. Where we used to be able to strain and recover in a 24 hour period, this is no longer possible. We must rest or pay a disproportionate price in prolonged fatigue. An inner adjustment is needed not only to the disabilities of the moment but also to the progressive physical deterioration which they forerun.

Olga Knopf, a 90 year old physician who has written extensively on aging, says that all the elderly suffer from periods of depression. Our western notions of "progress" have nothing to offer. *Any* life accomplishment loses significance when you realize your own extinction and death are approaching. There is no external achievement that by itself justifies the expenditure of life energy. Our spirit longs to create something that transcends time. But the body is more insistent than it has ever been that it must be dealt with.

The symptoms of aging are caused by the loss or malfunction of individual cells in every organ of the body. Biologically we know that death is necessary to preserve a species. Only by replacing individuals can a species adapt to a changing environment. Leonard Hayflick of Stanford University School of Medicine says that there is evidence that the life span of cells is somehow controlled from within. Other scientists dispute this and investigate "instructions" in the DNA molecule for errors that creep into the cell's production of protein or the existence of a death hormone that sabotages cells. As cells disappear, the tissues and muscles shrink, strength and endurance fade, impairing the ability to work. Skin wrinkles and tends to get flabby. The whole body shrinks and weight decreases. Nerves losing cells cannot transmit messages as rapidly as before or as accurately. Sight and hearing and all the senses weaken as a consequence. Every organ and function slows down, as does thought. Dark spots appear on the skin as cells fail to process wastes. Hair whitens as pigment is no longer manufactured and finally, co-ordination breaks down.

Deterioration is inevitable. No person escapes from it but many factors determine whether it will be fast or slow, partial or entire and whether it will have a greater or lesser influence on outer life as a whole. There are great differences between individuals of the same age. The burden of the body seems to count for less than the attitude adopted toward it. Resentment worsens infirmity.

We begin to feel "old" by means of other persons' reactions to us. We try to picture what we are through the vision that others have of us. It is unrealizable. Our vision does not coincide with any one of theirs. They all agree in their view that our face is that of an elderly person. For those who see us after a lapse of years, it has changed—for the worse; for those near to us, it is still our face. The sameness outweighs the change. For outsiders it is the ordinary face of a person of seventy-five or eighty. And what is it for us? We interpret our mirror cheerfully, angrily or with indifference according to our general attitude toward old age. Our inner being may not accept the label but in a certain sense we no longer know who we are. It is as if one had put on a borrowed mask or costume to play a new role. We are tempted to say, "I belong to a different category," when we see other older persons because we, too, first see them old and only from the outside. If one were sure of oneself, content with one's lot and on good terms with those around, age could remain theoretical were it not for the body awareness reminders.

The way in which we experience the day to day flow of time depends on what it holds, but as age advances, our subjective experience of time becomes compressed. Two consecutive summers are separated by an eternity for the child but as we age, the summers seem to follow each other with accelerating speed. There are indications that the speed of cellular mechanisms is inverted to time experience. Although time seems long to the child, her tissue reactions such as the healing of woulds are rapid. The reverse is true for the aged.

What is one to make of this? We all maintain a certain psychic continuity throughout our lives. Inside each one of us is much the same person who has been there from youth, despite the slower reaction time. But old age changes the individual's relation with time, with the world and with his own history. Moments become more precious.

"You must reach old age before you can understand the meaning—the splendid, absolute, unchallengeable, irreplaceable meaning of the word today!" Paul Claudel wrote in his eighties. And Mauriac in his journal said: "I do not feel detached from anyone or anything. But from now on, living will be enough to keep me occupied. This blood which still flows in the hand I lay on my knee, this sea that I feel beating within me, this transitory, not eternal ebb and flow, this world so close to its end—all these insist on being watched every moment, all these last moments before the very last." A more feminine and feeling point of view was expressed by Florida Scott-Maxwell: "Age puzzles me. I thought it was a quiet time. My seventies were interesting, and faily serene, but my eighties are passionate. I grow more intense as I age. To my own surprise I burst out with hot conviction...I must calm down. I am far too frail to indulge in moral fervour."[1]

The inner world of the very old is seldom worded. The authors quoted above were still in their eighties when their words were written. There may be weeks, months, even years of slow quiet gestation in the minds of quite old people. To speak of half-formed ideas which come with attunement to the inner self, is to destroy their growth. The very frailty of age guards its secrets. The conscious communicating mind is only a small part of the total psyche. The work that is going on may never be put into words but we have clues from the beginning of the aging process that it is occuring.

Somewhere in the sixties, memories, thoughts of the past, begin to compel attention, almost as if one is driven against one's will to relive the past accomplishments, mistakes and omissions of one's life. Childhood memories once repressed are relived. Images, fantasies, emotional attitudes—for a few moments you are back in the past. Then suddenly, you are not. You are in the now again with the years slipping by quickly. There seems to be an urge to learn what one has learned; to assess what one has achieved as well as to explore long forgotten misdeeds, as if there were some need to face squarely what one has been.

According to Robert Butler, psychiatrist and gerontologist, an old person is re-defining his identity when he reminisces about events everyone else has forgotten. This life review is a serious attempt to sift for nuggets of meaning, to attempt to resolve old doubts and conflicts that could never before be surveyed, to re-examine and restructure identity in terms of past and present experience.

Irene de Castellejo, old herself and speaking of her work with the aged, says that it is a fallacy that the old are necessarily lonely when alone. Some are, but not those quietly pondering and preparing, albeit without conscious intent, for death. They need long hours of solitude to round out their lives within. Many of the old are cheated of this essential solitude by the mistaken kindness of the young and their own unawareness of the need to be alone. We die alone. It is well to become accustomed to being alone before that moment comes. The old are generally too shielded, she feels. It is no kindness to the old to deprive them of their power still to grow. Olga Knopf agrees but more as a matter of practical management. "The more unnecessary assistance the old person gets, the more helpless he will become."[2]

This is *not* to say that the old person should be abandoned or isolated from warm family contacts but rather a warning against our "kindness" which is substituted for genuine affection and does not perceive the reality of the older person. Griefs do not shatter the old like the young. They have their tasks of assimilating the experience of earlier years. They must go back through their memories, re-collecting their past into a single whole—which in itself has a healing effect. If they are to die content, they must achieve the task of becoming completely the person they were meant to be.

The increasing strength of the earth powers of darkness, decay, and downgoing force the old to withdraw their attention from the outer world to the intense inner happenings of the mind. One has to return again and again to weep the unshed tears and to realize the innate knowledge which has been gained. We cannot feel all the grief of our many losses at the time we suffer them nor do we fully realize the meanings of the unexpected visions nor the dark regions of our inner being when we initially encounter them.

Simone de Beauvoir says "One must have lived a long time to have a true idea of the human condition, and to have a broad view of the way in which things happen: it is only then that one can 'foresee the present'—the task of the statesman. That is why in the course of history, elderly men have been entrusted with great responsibilities."[3] They have also been viewed as obstacles to progress. Each individual situation has its own context. However, in the inner experience of the elderly, two sets of values operate simultaneously; the desire to stay active and to maintain a sense of self worth in the eyes of others and the desire to withdraw from social commitments to a more leisurely, contemplative life.

The sociologist, Berniece Neugarten says the aged are more preoccupied with inner concerns and needs. They make few emotional commitments and have less interest in the outside world. They also experience a freedom from the obligation to respond as expected. Less energy is invested in pretending, in "niceness" or false emotions. It is interesting that this has survival value.

The Simontons who study cancer patients report the survivors are not the nice, polite, uncomplaining people, but the complainers, "selfish", assertive—in short, people who let themselves be themselves with their straight reactions. The feisty old man may not be too different in this sense from the wise old man or the wise old woman.

When we finally reach the time when we no longer compare our behaviour to standards of others outside ourselves, we may also be at a place when we can allow freedom of expression to the inner voice, a voice which speaks from the depths with none of our conscious concepts or sense of mortality. Rex Weaver, an Australian psychologist, says that when one "can do this without rational interference, he faces indeed his deeper reality which brings with it a feeling of immortality . . . that which existed before ego and that which goes beyond ego and points to ultimate but unknown things. It is as if one is not only this but also that which transcends this. In such a way we come to a knowledge of nature as she is and have touched upon that which underlies the phenomenal world."[4]

In his old age, Carl G. Jung spoke of these contents of the psyche: "The experience of the objective fact is all-important, because it denotes the presence of something which is not I, yet is still psychical. Such an experience can reach a climax where it becomes an experience of God. Even the smallest experience of that kind has a mana quality, a divine quality. It is fascinating. A bit more and it is the whole Deity, the giver of life. It is a decisive experience . . . " (C.G. Jung *Visions* seminars privately circulated)

Through this inner awareness you can come to understand more clearly the patterns and emotions you have lived and you glimpse the basis of the mystery of consciousness. In this way you go beyond time and space and move from the limitation of ways in which you have known yourself into the immortal drama. This is the borderland through which you move to physical death. Sandol Stoddard in her work on the Hospice movement says that we are aware of being imprisoned by the limitations of the ego and we hunger for something beyond. "Mystics have taught us for centuries that spirit takes only a temporal, restricted form in us while we dwell on earth; and that our five senses continually blunder, misinforming us and distracting our gaze from the essence of life which is holy and eternal. Time and space, they have insisted, should not be taken in the way we perceive them here and now, as practical measures of truth."[5] It is hard for the mystical point of view to gain a hearing in ordinary life but with the coming of age there is time again for wonder. Frances, a resident in a nursing home spoke of this:

> "I've been told that I must not succumb to the facts of my age. But why shouldn't I? I am now in my 91st year and I doubt that my activity for example, in civic af-

fairs, could restore my spirits to a state of bouncing bouyancy. Lack of physical strength alone keeps me inactive and often silent. I've been called senile. Senility is a convenient peg on which to hang non-conformity... A new set of faculties seems to be coming into operation. I seem to be awakening to a larger world of wonderment—to catch little glimpses of the immensity and diversity of creation. More than at any other time in my life, I seem to be aware of the beauties of our spinning planet and the sky above. I feel that old age sharpens my awareness."

Preparation for dying takes many forms, some of which we experience in earlier life. Mystical knowledge is prefigured when poetic experience enters into the dimension of death. Jacques Jiminez claims that all poetry is implicitly about dying. Ladislaus Boros[6] agrees that poetry is based in life and death. Within its discipline, man is called to live in proximity to the nature of things, to "dwell" in the earth. "It is the creation of being be means of words, the salvaging of true reality from confusion, the establishing of existence on its real basis; in short, the experience of the presence in our existence (in its integral reality) of death, and a sampling of death as our fully personal, perfect accomplishment." R.M. Rilke described poetic creation as the conservation and fitting together of a whole life's scattered experiences of meaning and lucidity.

To be a poet, therefore, means to separate from their context of day to day living the really important experiences one has had in the course of life and to express their relationship—the essential proximity of things, happenings and persons as they were grasped in the most lucid moments of being. Apparently this corresponds to the essential task we have in preparing for death. To T.S. Eliot dying was a process of transformation and transcendence continually happening during our earthly life:

What we call the beginning is often the end
And to make an end is to make a beginning...
We shall not cease from exploration
And the end of all our exploring
Will be to arrive where we started
And know the place for the first time...

It was his perception that biological death was merely the annihilation of the final set of barriers between man and God, "costing not less than everything."

By definition no one can report to us the actual experience of death but there exist reports from individuals who have clinically "died" and, because of modern resuscitation techniques, recovered. Elizabeth Kubler-Ross, M.D., describes some in her research and Raymond A. Moody, Jr., M.D.[7] reports on 150 people who, having been pronounced biologically dead, were "brought back to life". All reported the experience of dying as something like a journey out of space and time in an indescribable spiritual body "something like an energy pattern". Moody's subjects often reported the presence of spiritual companions and told of going through dark tunnel-like spaces on their way to brilliant, blazing light. Once they merged into the presence of a "being of light" whose love for them was "overwhelming and indescribable", they each felt a tremendous radiance and joy.

> "I was out of my body, there's no doubt about it, because I could see my own body there on the operating room table. My soul was out! All this made me feel very bad at first, but then this really bright light came... from the moment the light spoke to me, I felt really good—secure and loved. The love which come from it is just unimaginable, indescribable."

said one subject. And, another:

> "I floated... up into this pure crystal light... It was beautiful and so bright, so radiant, but it didn't hurt my eyes. It's not any kind of light you can describe on

earth. I didn't actually see a person in this light and yet
it has a special identity . . . "

Religious people tended to describe the being of light in
their own tradition as an angel, Jesus, or God but even firm
atheists, Dr. Moody reports, perceived it as some sort of
religious figure. All subjects reported feeling powerfully
changed by the experience., lifted to new levels of consciousness in which mind and spirit took new precedence
over the material. Most said they had also undergone an
experience of a miraculously rapid review of actions and
events from their entire life. It resembled the Judgement of
ancient Egyptian, Tibetan and medieval Christian traditions but was done in a wholly loving way. Mistakes were
demonstrated as if one could learn from them.

Many of the experiences reported correspond to
those found in writings over 2000 years old. The differences
are mainly cultural and connected with different ideas
about the purpose of human life in space and time. All see
death as a journey. The Tibetan Book of the Dead was
designed to be read to the dying person and for several days
after his death. As interpreted by Dr. Carl G. Jung, it
teaches that the dying person sees a brilliant light almost
immediately at the moment of death. He goes through a
series of struggles after this which represent various levels
of spiritual development coming under attack from worldly
illusions. Escape from the fate of reincarnation can only
happen if the illusions are resisted but then one enters
Samadhi, the Clear Light of the Void.

Medieval Christians, although not believing in reincarnation, also had instruction manuals for the dying
which emphsized the necessity for confession of sins and
death of egoistic desires before one could come into the
immediate presence of God. Most religious groups of the
world agree that the manner of death is deeply important.
Suicide for instance, is seen as extremely destructive, if not

fatal to the soul.

The classical Christian definition of death—the separation of body and soul—in recent years has been the subject of further theological thought. Karl Rahner[8], for example, takes the traditional Christian position that the soul, the spiritual life principle of man, does not perish when the structure of the body is dissolved but maintains its proper life in some wholly different manner of existence and he raises the questions doctrine has left unanswered. For instance, does the soul separate herself from the body as a result of her own deeper dynamics or is she separated from it as an accident in opposition to her innate tendency. Just as the body components break down and reassemble in other forms of organic and inorganic matter, does the soul through substantial union with the body as her essential form, also have a relationship to this radical oneness of the universe? Now at death, no longer bound to an individual body structure does she enter into a much closer, more intimate relationship to the universe as a whole?—that is to say, does she unite with the basic oneness by which all things in the world are related and mutually influence each other?

Rahner thinks that certain parapsychological phenomena, now puzzling, might be more readily and naturally explained if the soul has always possessed an all-cosmic relationship which becomes a real possibility for her only in death. The entire world does not become the "body" of this particular soul but rather "by surrendering her limited bodily structure in death, (she) becomes open toward the 'all' and, in some way, a co-determining factor of the universe precisely in its character as the ground for the personal life of other spiritual-corporeal beings." ...This hypothesis would also render more readily intelligible the doctrine of purgatory. That doctrine implies a further maturing of man, even after death..."[9]

Both Eastern and Western traditions have much to teach us about the process of dying and its tremendous potential for personal growth whatever the structure of our religious or philosophical beliefs. At the time of dying, the individual needs the kind of time and space that is concerned only with the process of giving and receiving human care and connectedness; she needs an empathetic acceptance of this time of closing or of passage. For this reason, the Hospice Movement has flourished in the last few years. Hospices all over the country now receive federal funding, including Medicare, and are being unanimously praised by physicians, clergy and health care experts. Hospice helps terminally ill patients to face death without pain or fear by using highly sophisticated techniques of pain and symptom control while refusing to adopt "heroic" methods of resuscitation in inappropriate situations.

How we experience death, even under the best of circumstances, is deeply individual and "dread-full" without question. We all have to know that we have kept the presence of death at bay and our own presence from the dying. The process of dying needs to be gotten out of the hospitals and back into the home and the midst of family, neighborhood, friends. True, if this were to become more common, ministers, priests and rabbis might have on their hands a great many shattered families and relatives. But for once they would be shattered by confrontation with reality, by the claims of the dying not to be deserted, not to be denied human presence. As Peter Berger has pointed out, the sealing up of metaphysical concerns is one of the baneful aspects of our adolescent society.

Most religious and philosophical traditions teach that awareness of death—one's own death—is the best possible preparation for living. Knowing that you are going to die, you refuse to fritter away your time on nonsense, you drop your masks, your little vanities and false ambitions—you dare to say exactly what you mean. To live fully is to embrace life in all its transformations. To the extent that we realize this, we glimpse what a more highly conscious human society might become.

FOOTNOTES

* Few writers have entered the last fifth of a century of possible life and attempted to convey its day by day realities. The initial segment of this essay is a paraphrase of insights from Olga Knopf's successful aging: *The Facts and Falacies of Growing Old*, Florida Scott Maxwell's *The Measure of My Days* and talks with my father John F. Dinger, now 80.

1. Scott-Maxwell, Florida. *Measure of My Days*

2. Knopf, Olga. *Successful Aging: The Facts and Fallacies of Growing Old*

4. Weaver, Rex. *The Wise Old Woman: A Study of Active Imagination*, London: Vincent Stuart LTD. 1964.

5. Stoddard, Sandol. *The Hotspice Movement: a Better Way of Caring for the Dying*, New York: Stein and Day Publishers; 1978, p.203

6. *Boros, Ladislaus. The Mystery of Death*, New York: Seabury Press; 1972, p.63

7. Moody, Raymond A.. *Life After Life*, Atlanta: 1975

8. Rahner, Karl. *On the Theology of Death*, New York: Herder and Herder, 1964

9. Rahner, Karl. *Ibid.*

DYING AND DEATH

Charles A. Garfield, Ph.D.

People have thought about life and death since Neanderthal times. The fact that "Living with Death" was a cover story of *Newsweek*[1] and that *Time*[2] did a feature story on "A Better Way of Dying" indicates the extent to which dying and death have become concerns to the lay public as well as the health professionals - a surprising development for a culture so often described as death denying. There are a number of reasons for this increasing awareness. Recent advances in innovative medical technology are significantly altering the nature of dying, often compelling the terminally ill to confront years of chronic illness before the actual moment of death. In addition, many postindustrial Americans are alienated from traditional family, religious, and community supports. The results are increased by loneliness, anxiety, and self-doubt. Feifel[3] observes that it is a historic phenomenon that consciousness of death becomes more acute during periods of social disorganization, when individual choice tends to replace automatic conformity to consensual social values. He states:

> With the advent of the H-bomb, physical science has presently made it possible for us all to share a common epitaph. Not only descendance in social immortality

but history as well is being menaced. Time along with space can now be annihilated. Even celebration of the tragic will be beyond our power. Death is becoming a wall.

Death also has become more difficult to deal with because of its expulsion from daily life. Dying and death are now the responsibility of the "professional" (i.e., physician, nurse, clergyman, and funeral director). Unfortunately, many of us use our technical expertise as a defense against our own death-related anxieties.

Care of the Dying

As physicians, nurses, and allied professionals perfect their skill at providing care and support for the terminally ill, we must continually be aware of the enormity of the emotional trauma confronting our dying patients and their families. It is interesting to realize the word "care" drives from the Gothic *kara*, which means "to lament, to grieve, to experience sorrow, to cry out with." Nouwen[4] notes that "we tend tolook at carying as an attitude of the strong toward the weak, of the powerful toward the powerless, the haves toward the have nots." We often experience great discomfort when we are invited to enter into someone's pain before we have done something about it. But distant concern appears strangely antithetical to the basic component of caring, namely, empathy—the more expressive German translation of which is "Einfuhlung," meaning "to feel oneself into." Nouwen continues with the observation that

> when we honestly ask ourselves which persons in our lives mean the most to us, we often find that it is those who instead of giving much advice, solutions, or cures, have chosen rather to share our pain and touch our wounds with a gentle and tender hand. The friend who can be silent with us in a moment of despair or confusion, who can stay with us in an hour of grief and bereavement, who can tolerate not knowing, not curing, not healing and face with us the reality of our powerlessness, that is the friend who cares.

In as emotionally charged an environment as exists in most of our contact with seriously ill patients and their families, attempts at decreased emotional involvement are frequently experienced by patients as painful abandonment. These attempts to remain objective are born of the notion that to become emotionally accessible to one's patients implies a loss of scientific objectivity, a compromising of rational judgment, and a decrease in the time-effective management of one's caseload. When communicated to our students and younger practitioners, this bias serves largely to disallow authentic human communication between helper and patient and prevents the next generation of health providers from mastering the art as well as the science of patient care.

To understand the nature of effective support for dying patients and their families, as health providers we must:

1. Realize that role models appropriate to laboratory science are largely inappropriate to the effective emotional support of patients and families facing life-threatening illness. That is, we *are* emotionally involved with our patients and we need to be able to discuss this involvement with our patients and our colleagues in order to maximize the supportive nature of these basically interdependent relationships.

2. Recognize that the psychosocial aspects of patient care require a great deal more than "hand holding." Almost without exception, physicians who take the psychological and social issues surrounding life-threatening illness seriously can develop a real mastery of this increasingly important aspect of patient care.

3. Examine carefully our own attitudes concerning death and the dying patient and realize that when it comes to a subjective understanding of the nature of the dying process, most patients know a great deal more than those who care for them.

As health professionals, we are often involved in situations in which we are like lifeguards watching our patients flounder in the water several hundred yards off shore. Perhaps the distressed person does not know how to swim or, knowing how, simply does not have enough strength to make it to shore.

> Our professional lifeguards, it seems, do not know how to swim themselves. To be sure, they have been given extensive training in many life-saving techniques, all of which they have tested in the children's pool. The know how to row a boat; they know how to throw out a ring buoy; they know how to give artificial respiration. But they do not know how to swim themselves. They cannot save another because, given the same circumstances, they could not save themselves.[5]

Many of our attempts to understand the emotional realities of dying patients and their families are doomed to failure because we base our approaches on a set of faulty operational assumptions:

1. We rely on summary information about the patient's emotional world, that is, notes in the chart of brief word-of-mouth explanations.

2. Our values as health professionals are most often firmly rooted in middle-class thinking, making it difficult to comprehend cross-cultural variation in value systems.

3. We are unable to effectively incorporate or interpret experiential and behavioral extremes in a meaningful fashion.

4. We have great difficulty in dealing with emotional expression (for example, extreme anger, long-term depression, etc.). The somewhat presumptuous yet frequently invoked assessment of the patient's chosen form of expression as "inappropriate affect" is often a signal of our own inability to cope.

5. We attempt to deal reasonably with what is most often— from the patient's perspective—an unreasonable life situation.

Our efforts to ignore or disqualify emotional expression,

make decisions on the basis of cursory and most often superficial data, and eliminate extremes from the dying patient's emotional life are usually perfectly reasonable yet superficial. Our effectiveness will increase in direct proportion to our capacity to acknowledge the great range of quite normal emotional responses to life-threatening illness and the complexities of psychological functioning and assessment. Increased effectiveness results when we continue to be present to our patients in spite of the fact that the greater portion of their psychological functioning remains a mystery to us.

Feelings about death and the process of dying, like feelings about huamn sexuality, are very intimate concerns that most people are unwilling to share with those constrained by the scientific rigors of a tightly designed research protocol. As one elderly man dying of lung cancer stated, "I'll be damned if I share my feelings about dying and death with anyone who makes two-minute U-turns at the foot of my bed." To date, no research or systematic clinical observation has verified any preprogrammed set of stages in the dying process; that is, researchers and practitioners have not empirically identified any set of linear, unidirectional, and invariant stages. Certainly, many patients who are dying exhibit denial, anger, bargaining, depression, and occasionally acceptance,[6] but it is innaccurate to suppose that all individuals, regardless of belief system, age, race, culture, and historical period, die in a uniform sequence. It is more likely that existing theoretical frameworks become self-fulfilling prophecies, imposed by health professionals who may coerce the dying person into conforming with a powerfully suggestive typology. All too frequently I have heard health professionals talk about "forcing a patient to move from stage three (bargaining) to stage four (depression) because the patient's condition was deteriorating so fast that he or she might not have time to reach stage five (acceptance)." To needlessly add one more ponderous agenda to a patient's already heavily burdened psyche in an injustice to all concerned. Out of respect and appreciation for Elizabeth Kubler-Ross and her work, I must note that she has made this point many times herself. With regard to all our theoretical models, I am reminded of Aristotle's observation: "Dear is Plato, but dearer still is truth."

In my own research, the major issues identified by the dying patient are (1) that he will become quietly isolated because of a decrease in communication resulting from the unwillingness of those responsible for his care to maintain the openness and emotional support essential for him to live out his life with some hope and participation in meaningful relationships; (2) that he will be subjected to painful, uncomfortable, and demanding procedures that might prolong existence without prolonging a desirable quality of life, and that the disease will force him to endure intense, chronic pain seemingly without end; and (3) that loss of control of bodily, interpersonal, and cognitive functions will compel him to confront a terrifying and alien set of experiences, stripped of all decision-making powers.

I have found the following outline useful in determining and meeting the psychosocial needs of terminal patients.

1. With the assistance of the patient, define the major areas of emotional distress.
2. Respond to the patient's requests for information with an honest, complete, and presentation of the major aspects of illness and treatment.
3. Inform the patient's family of the status of his health so that family members can assume their rightful status as members of the treatment team.
4. Make it possible for the patient to be aware of staff expectations concerning treatment, patient-staff relationships, etc., and conversely for the staff to be aware of patient expectations.
5. Always compare your perceptions of the patient and his

situation with those of your colleagues. It is hazardous to make unilateral judgements about another person's emotional reality.

6. Remember that psychosocial evaluation, like medical appraisal, is a continuous process. Two innovations that have proven successful in maintaining ongoing evaluation are (a) the institution of interdisciplinary psychosocial rounds, the specific purpose of which is to evaluate staff success in meeting the emotional needs of all patients (the option of inviting patients to talk to staff about how best to care for them has been a successful aspect of these rounds); and (b) the use of a psychosocial log in which all health providers may record their feelings and thoughts on various aspects of working with seriously ill patients. This log can serve as a catalyst for discussion during psychosocial rounds.

Hospice and Counseling Programs

Two important and creative responses to the needs of dying patients and their families have been the development of the hospice concept and volunteer counseling programs modled after the SHANTI Project in the San Francisco Bay area. Pioneered successfully throughout England and other European countries, the hospice is seen by some as a major medical innovation in the United States and Canada. SHANTI Project volunteers currently number more than one hundred and are donating nearly 50,000 hours of counseling time per year.

In its most general sense, the hospice is a program that provides palliative and supportive care for terminally ill patients and their families. Originally a medieval name for a way station where pilgrims and travelers could be replenished and cared for, hospice in its current usage denotes a more humane philosophy of care and an organized program of support for dying patients and their families.

Liegner[7] notes that the key principle of hospice care is reduction of pain; by pain he means not only physical pain but also psychic pain. The reduction of pain in a hospice is effected through several strategies:

* Polypharmacy—the practice of administering medication in doses adequate to keep the patient's pain always below the pain threshold
* Humane treatment and environment
* Psychological and pastoral counseling
* Special attention at the moment of death
* Social services for the bereaved

Ideally, hospices rely on a core of dedicated staff and volunteers. All health providers, physicians, nurses, and auxiliary staff are encouraged to listen carefully to the patient and to share their observations with other staff in the hope of more successfully meeting the physical and emotional needs of the patient.

Projects modeled after the SHANTI Project, often referred to as volunteer hospice programs, are appearing in many parts of the United States and abroad. Requests for volunteer counseling, companionship, and emotional support come from patients, family members, survivors of a death, and members of the health professions. Volunteers provide services to clients free of charge with primary allegiance to the client rather than to any single institutional setting. The project is committed to providing continuity of care for all clients; thus, volunteers continue to work with their clients in the home, general hospital, or extended care facility. After a rigorous screening and selection process, SHANTI Project volunteers go through a comprehensive training program and make a commitment to work at least one year with the project for a period of eight to ten hours per week. A training film for physicians and nurses, "Counseling the Terminally Ill," focusing largely on the work of the SHANTI Project, has been produced under the sponsorship of the National Institute of Mental Health.

National Hospice Organization
765 Prospect Street
New Haven, Connecticut 06511

SHANTI Project
106 Evergreen Lane
Berkeley, California 94705

Near-Death Experiences

A man is dying and, as he reaches the point of greatest physical distress, he hears himself pronounced dead by his doctor. He begins to hear an uncomfortable noise, a loud ringing or buzzing, and at the same time feels himself moving very rapidly through a long dark tunnel. After this he suddenly finds himself outside his own physical body but still in the immediate physical environment, and he sees his own body from a distance, as though he is a spectator. He watches the resuscitation attempt from this unusual vantage point and is in a state of emotional upheaval.

After a while, he collects himself and becomes more accustomed to his odd condition. He notices that he still has a body, but one of a very different nature and with very different powers from the physical body he has left behind. Soon other things begin to happen. Others come to meet and help him. He glimpses the spirits of relatives and friends who have already died, and a loving, warm spirit of a kind he has never encountered before—a being of light—appears before him. This being asks him a question, nonverbally, to make him evaluate his life, and helps him along by showing him a panoramic, instantaneous play back of the major events of his life.

At some point he finds himself approaching some sort of barrier or border, apparently representing the limit between earthly life and the next life. Yet, he finds that he must go back to the earth, that the time for his death has not yet come. At this point he resists, for by now he is taken up with his experiences in the afterlife and does not want to return. He is overwhelmed by intense feelings of joy, love, and peace. Despite his attitude, he somehow reunites with his physical body and lives.[8]

Raymond Moody, Jr., distilled the "normative" near-death experience described above from the 150 anecdotal reports published in his book, *Life After Life*.[9] Moody's composite contains the experiential elements most frequently reported by people in his sample who "had either been resuscitated after being pronounced dead, faced imminent death through injury or illness, or been with individuals who relayed their own experiences as they were dying".[10] Most fascinating is his observation that these experiences occurred independently of both the individual differences among patients and the events and circumstances that resulted in their brush with death. From his analysis of the data, Moody concluded that the near-death experience profoundly alters a person's consciousness.

Karlis Osis and Erlender Haraldsson[11] compiled the death-bed observatory doctors and nurses in the United States and India made of nearly five hundred dying patients. The most common experience reported by dying patients in his sample had visions of a religious figure or a deceased loved one who came to escort the dying person to another realm.

The near-death experiences reported in the medical and psychological literatures do not appear to be "positive proof of life after death" but rather altered-state experiences not at all specific to the dying process. I have received several letters from women who, in natural childbirth, had very similar experiences. I believe that the near-death experiences described by Moody, Osis and Haraldsson, and others are a subclass of a larger group of altered-state experiences attainable through a variety of techniques and circumstances. In the past two years, I have worked with

173 cancer patients who have subsequently died. I spent an average of three to four hours per week with them for a period ranging from several weeks to almost two years. Among the 21 percent who told one of their altered-state experiences, four groups emerged.

The first group experienced a powerful white light and celestial music (as in Moody's accounts) as well as an encounter with a religious figure or deceased relative (similar to that reported by Osis and Haraldsson). The patients described these as "incredibly real, peaceful, and beautiful." A second group experienced demonic figures, nightmarish images of great lucidity. A third reported dream-like images, sometimes "blissful," sometimes "terifying," sometimes alternating. The images were not nearly so lucid as those related by the first two groups. However, they appeared to have as great a variation in content. The fourth group experienced the void or a tunnel or both. That is, the patients reported drifting endlessly in outer space or being encapsulated in a limited environment with obvious spatial constraints. A common theme in their accounts was the contrast between maximal freedom and miximal constraint with, in some cases, fluctuation from one to the other.

My work has included interviews with individuals who have had near-death experiences or who have been pronounced clinically dead and then revived. In an effort to evaluate the anectodal reports of Moody, Kubler-Ross, and others, I conducted in-depth interviews with seventy-two intensive-care or coronary-care patients. Since my primary function is to provide basic emotional support, I was often the first person to interact with the patient for an appreciable length of time after his brush with death. My contact occurred anywhere from three hours to two days after the indident. Thirty-six patients reported no memory of the event at all. Their last memory before losing consciousness was of being in their hospital room and when they awoke they were either in the ICU or CCU "hooked up to the hardware." Fourteen reported experiences similar to those collected by Moody, Kubler-Ross, and Osis, including seeing a bright light, hearing "celestial" music, and meeting religious figures or deceased relatives. Eight reported lucid visions of a demonic or nightmarish nature. Eight reported having dreamlike images, four of which were entirely positive and the other four alternating between positive and negative. Six patients reported drifting endlessly in outer space among the planets, cut loose as if thrown from a space ship. No significant changes in content were expressed by any of the patients in three interviews conducted at weekly intervals after the event.

In light of this research, three main observations seem important. First, it appears that not everyone dies a blissful, accepting death. Recently my friend died. Her tortuous, labored breathing during the final twenty-four hours hardly appeared blissful. I hope those who suggest that she was really "feeling no pain" thanks to the "immunity" of the comatose state or because she was really "out of her body" are correct. However, almost as many of the dying patients I interviewed reported negative visions (encounters with demonic figures, etc.) as reported blissful experiences.

Second, Pelletier and Garfield[12] note that context is a powerful variable in such altered-state experiences as the hypnotic, meditative, psychedelic, and schizophrenic. In keeping with the early LSD research, we might very well find that a caring environment including supportive family, friends, and staff is an important factor in maximizing the likelihood of a positive altered-state experience for the dying. Certainly helping dying patients relate to their experiences in a constructive fashion rather than imposing psychiatric judgment is the more supportive stance. Whatever they represent, those experiences were very important to the dying patients who had them. We need to examine more carefully the impact of context on the dying process, including the quality of advocacy and nonjudgmental caring offered by family and staff. Contextual as well as psychobiological factors may significantly influence the altered-state experiences of the dying patient.

The third observation is, as Kastenbaum[13] notes:

> The happily, happily theme threatens to draw attention away from the actual situations of the dying person, their loved ones and their care givers over the days, weeks, and months preceding death. What happens up to the point of that fabulous transition from life to death recedes into the background. This could not be more unfortunate.

Will our aversion to death take yet another form and leave us prey to promises of life after death that we cannot integrate emotionally? It is certainly feasible that we run the risk of once again denying death and perhaps biasing our level of care to those who are dying. Will our "knowledge of life after death" leave us in a position to "abandon life-saving efforts for some people, try less hard to save lives at critical moments"[12]

Conclusion

> It is hard to have patience with people who say "There is no death" or "death doesn't matter." There is death, and whatever happens has consequences, and it and they are irrevocable and irreversible. You might as well say that birth doesn't matter. I look up at the night sky. Is anything more certain than that in all those vast times and spaces, if I were allowed to search them, I should nowhere find her face, her voice, her touch? She died. She is dead. Is the word so difficult to learn?[15]

C.S. Lewis astutely observes that whether we view death as annihilation or transition it is a real and often monumental event, an emotional blow associated with a change of form. Those I love in the form I love no longer exist. Those having near-death experiences exuberantly extol the virtues of loving and caring for one's fellow man. So let us have the courage to realize that death often will be a bitter pill to swallow. Our pain will almost always accompany the deaths of those we most love. Our wish will almost always be that help and caring are available.

> Real care is not ambiguous. Real care excludes indifference and is the opposite of apathy. The word "care" finds its roots in the Gothic "kara," which means "to lament." The basic meaning of care is: to grieve, to experience sorrow, to cry out with. I am very much struck by this background of the word care, because we tend to look at caring as an attitude of the strong toward the weak, of the powerful toward the powerless, of the haves toward the have-nots. And, in fact, we feel quite uncomfortable with an invitation to enter into someone's pain before doing something about it . . . Still, when we honestly ask ourselves which persons in our lives mean the most to us, we often find that it is those who, instead of giving much advice, solutions, or cures, have chosen rather to share our pain and touch our wounds with a gentle and tender hand. The friend who can be silent with us in a moment of despair of confusion, who can tolerate not knowing, not curing, not healing and face with us the reality of our powerlessness, that is the friend who cares . . . Our tendency is to run away from the painful realities or to try to change them as soon as possible. But cure without care makes us into rulers, controllers, manipulators, and prevents a real community from taking shape. Cure without care makes us preoccupied with quick changes, impatient and unwilling to share each other's burden. And so cure can often become offending instead of liberating. It is therefore not so strange that cure is not seldom refused by people in need . . . Those who can sit in silence with their fellow man not knowing what to say but knowing that they should be there, can bring new life in a dying heart. Those who are not afraid to hold a hand in gratitude, to shed tears in grief, and to let a sigh of distress arise straight from the heart can break through paralyzing boundaries and witness the birth of a new fellowship, the fellowship of the broken. [16]

FOOTNOTES

1. Newsweek; May 1, 1978.

2. Time; June 5, 1978.

3. Feifel, Herman. *New Meanings of Death*. New York: McGraw-Hill, 1977.

Nouwen, Henri. *Out of Solitude*. Notre Dame, Ind.: Ave Maria Press, 1974.

5. Carkhuff, R., and Berenson, B. *Beyond the Counseling and Therapy*. New York: Holt, Rinehart and Winston, 1967.

6. Kubler-Ross, Elizabeth. *On Death and Dying*. New York: Macmillian, 1969.

7. Liegner, L. St. Christopher's hospice, care of the dying patient. *Journal of the American Medical Association*, 1974. 234, 1047-1048.

8. Goleman, D. *Back From The Brink*. Psychology Today, April 1977. 10, 56-59.

9. *Moody, Raymond. Life After Life*. Atlanta: Mockingbird Books, 1975.

10. Goleman, *Ibid*.

11. Osis, Karlis, and Haraldsson, Erlender. *At the Hour of Death*. New York: Avon Books, 1977.

12. Pelletier, Kenneth R., and Garfield, Charles. *Consciousness East and West*. New York: Harper and Row, 1976.

13. Kastenbaum, Robert. Temptations from the ever after. *Human Behavior, 1977*. 6(1), 28-33.

14. Kastenbaum, *Ibid*.

15. Lewisl C.S. *A Grief Observed*. New York: Seabury Press, 1963.

16. Nouwen, *Ibid*.

ANNOTATED BIBLIOGRAPHY

Becker, Ernest. The Denial of Death. New York: The Free Press, 1973.

In the first three chapters of this Pultizer Prize-winning work, the author develops the thesis that man's innate fear of death is a principal source of his activity. In brilliant fashion, he develops the notion that the suppression of our innate vulnerability provides our major source of energy. Although the remainder of the book covers such topics as mental illness and especially the psychoanalytic theories of Otto Rank, the initial section is one of the best analyses of the relationship among dying, death, and the human condition.

de Beauvoir, Simone. A Very Easy Death. Harmondsworth: Penguin Books, 1969.
An insightful and moving account of her mother's death. I recommend it for its accurate description of the inexorable humiliation of a proud woman during a dying process that was far more tortuous than easy. The daughter's conflicting experiences of anger and affection in the face of her mother's death are superb and constitute an exposition of some of the experiences of a prototypic survivor.

Feifel, Herman (Ed.). New Meanings of Death. New York: McGraw-Hill, 1977.
This anthology is an update of the editor's influential work, *The Meaning of Death*, published in 1959. It examines the historical, sociological, psychological, developmental, and clinical aspects of death and dying. Some of the leaders in the field examine such topics as death and development through the life span, meanings of death to children, death and the physician, nurses and the human experience of dying, preparation for death, death education, and the relationship of death to immortality, the law, and poetry. This is an interesting collection of papers suitable for students, academicians, and clinicians.

Garfield, Charles A. Psychosocial Care of the Dying Patient. New York: McGraw-Hill, 1978.

This anthology is directed specifically at all physicians, nurses, and allied health professionals who work with dying patients and their families. It is intended as a resource text for clinicians to assist in identifying the emotional needs of the dying patient and family and to suggest helpful ways of providing the necessary support. A more ambitious intent is to identify the entire area of basic emotional support for patients and families as a legitimate and vital concern for any fully competent health professional. Topics covered include guidelines for terminal patient care, patients and families facing life-threatening illness, doctor-patient relationships, psychological needs of the terminally ill, counseling the patient's family, bioethical issues, the development of the SHANTI Project and the hospice movement.

Garfield, Charles A. Stress and Survival: The Emotional Realities of Life-Threatening Illness. St. Louis: Mosby, 1979.

This anthology is intended for physicians, nurses, and allied health professionals who provide support for patients and families facing life-threatening illness. A basic premise of the book is that one or more such supportive presences can markedly influence the patient's level of stress, will to live, and possibility of survival. The primary purposes of the book are: (1) in the words of Terrence Des Pres in his book *The Survivor*, "To understand the capacity of men and women to live beneath the pressure of protracted crisis, to sustain terrible damage in mind and body, and yet be there, sane, alive, still human"; (2) to offer insights into the ways that emotional support may be instrumental in promoting quality of life, longevity, and, at times, survival; and (3) to examine closely the optimal ways of providing emotional support to patients and families facing life-threatening illness. The topics include psychosocial elements of survival, the relation of social and psychological factors to illness, new dimensions in the alleviation of stress, emotional impact on health professional and patient, personal encounters with life-threatening illness, the chronically ill child, understanding pain and suffering, and care of the dyir patient.

Glaser, Barney, and Struss, Anselm. Awareness of Dying. Chicago: Aldine, 1965.

The best of the sociological studies available on the subject of dying. The data gathered for this book came from considerable field work in a variety of hospital settings. Perhaps the most important theoretical concept is that of varying contexts of awareness of death that exist in the hospital social system. This book will be of interest to hospital clinicians interested in understanding the impact of the hospital itself on staff, patients, and families.

Kastenbaum, Robert, and Aisenberg, Ruth. The Psychology of Death. New York: Springer Publishing, 1972.

This book is one of the most informative and interesting on the psychology of death. It is a scholarly work that combines original thought and the best research and thinking available. It contains enlightening analyses of historical, cultural, societal, developmental, and clinical issues involved in understanding the psychological aspects of dying and death.

Kubler-Ross, Elizabeth. On Death and Dying. New York: Macmillan, 1969.

This popular work has had more circulation than any other book in the field. It is a caring and humane analysis of the needs of the dying patient with practical advice for all those who provide care. Although Dr. Kubler-Ross's "five stage" model has been repudiated by most major thinkers in the field, this book should be regarded as a helpful and compassionate guide for clinicians.

Lewis, C.S. A Grief Observed. New York: Seabury Press, 1963.

"No one ever told me that grief felt so much like fear." So begins an extraordinarily honest and revealing expose of the grief of this well-known writer-philosopher. Originally written as a self-therapy journal without plans for publication, this powerful little book provides a superb first-hand account of the existential and emotional plight of an individual who has lost the most important person in his world. I highly recommend this book as a resource in providing a humane balance to the more clinical literature on grief and bereavement.

Lund, Doris. Eric. Philadelphia: J.B. Lippincott, 1974.

This book is the product of a mother's ardous task of writing about the death of her seventeen-year-old son from acute leukemia. It is an inspiring and lovingly written story of a boy who challenged his illness and its insidious effects by living powerfully and creatively in the face of death. It will be of assistance to those clinicians who need to understand the plight of the parent in life-threatening illness and also provides a balance to the more detached clinical literature.

Parkes, Colin Murray. Bereavement. New York: Penguin, 1972.

This work is the result of a comprehensive study of adult grief and its impact. It is a scholarly work of use to those interested in more than a clinical distillation of grief reactions and their symptoms. Included are suggestions for helping the bereaved and understanding the psychological processes involved in coping with the loss of a loved one.

Rosenthal, Ted. How Could I Not Be Among You? New York: Braziller, 1973.

This is a collection of some extremely moving poetry and prose from Ted Rosenthal, a Berkeley poet, who discovered at the age of thirty that he was dying of acute leukemia. He powerfully shares the emotional realities confronting the dying patient by examining his life in general. At rock bottom, he becomes aware of the psychic outrageousness of "ceasing to be" and the emotionally unfathomable question, "How could I not be among you?" This book is highly recommended for anyone attempting to understand the existential drama confronting the dying patient.

Shneidman, Edwin. Deaths of Man. New York: Quadrangle/New York Times, 1973.

An extremely well-written analysis of death including some innovative ideas of considerable interest. This is a psychologically sophisticated work of interest to scholars and others interested in the impact and the implications of death for the human psyche. The author includes some of his own concepts such as survivor-victims and their assistance by postvention, subintentioned death, and the effects of megadeath.

Weisman, Avery. On Dying and Denying. New York: Behavioral Publications, 1972.

This scholarly work, based on some of the best research available, concentrates on the central role of denial in the dying process. The book contains some excellent clinical case material and is best suited for those with more than an elementary understanding of psychological processes.